Lighten Up and Live Longer

A Collection of
Jokes, Anecdotes, and
Stories Guaranteed to
Tickle Your Soul

H.F. Brigham
Free Public Library
P.O. Box 5
Bakersfield, VT 05441

Sue Baldwin

Insights Training and Consulting
Stillwater, Minnesota

© 1999 by Sue Baldwin

All rights reserved.
Cover and Book Design by Ronna Hammer
Production by Román Soto
Edited by Mary Steiner Whelan

ISBN 0-9654439-1-4

Published by:
Insights Training & Consulting
2559 Hawthorne Lane
Stillwater, MN 55082-5266

Phone and fax: 651-439-4100
Web site: www.suebaldwin.com
E-mail: baldwin@visi.com

Printed in the United States of America

This book is dedicated to my two grandchildren,
Nicholas Timothy and Anna Christine Scheel. They give
my life meaning and intensify my desire to
live a full and healthy life.

Table of Contents

Acknowledgments

I would like to thank the following people who made contributions to this book. Without the support of these people, this book would still be in production—rather than in your hands.

Gayle Ahlgren
Ruth Appleton
Carrie Baldwin
Lauren Behl
Vicki Bliss
Mary Chapman
Chuck Desnick
Michelle Emerling
David Goodwin
Ruth Goodwin
Lori Hameister
Lynne Hicks
Kim Ulrich Johnson
Angela Lillie
Brad Lyman
Traci Lyman
Deb Marvin

Mary Miller
Heidi Presslein
Kim Richman
Terri Russell
Heather Sanders
Kris Scheel
Susan Scheel
Dennis Slusher
Cheryl Smith
Chris Smith
Judy Sporer
Susan Stenberg
Julie Thole
Leslie Thomas
Teresa Thompson
Sandy Walz
Mary Joy Zawislakoski

To the following people who added their personal drawings to enhance the creativity of this book.

Meeghan Meyer Andersen	Olivia Lyman
Emma Allen	Alisha Pepera
Jenni Allison	Devin Peters
Carrie Baldwin	Mackie Purst
Lairen Balker	Breana Ramirez
Kelly Bergeson	Roxanne Robinson
Alexander David Bick	Amanda Russell
Vicki Bliss	Jake Sandor
D. J. Brown	Tim Scheel
Grazelle Burns	Joe Sletten
Maureen Carolan	Heather Schmidt
Jean Dunn	Nicole Schmidt
Sofia Valencia Ellefson	Nicole Stiff
Libby Ewing	Seth Spawn
Alyse Finley	Courtney Sprain
Brad Gilbert	Grace Tilka
David Goodwin	Kaitlyn Wasleske
Lauren Hedlund	Leah Weipert
Alyson Heroff	Kelly Wrobel
Heather Johnson	Francesca Zeller
Karen Lyman	
Lanie Lyman	Cover artwork: Peter Blunck

Mary Steiner Whelan, who offered me support and encouragement as an editor, fellow author, and traveling companion.

Ronna Hammer and Román Soto, who used their expertise and creativity to design and lay out this book.

Andrea McCready and Teresa Hudoba for their editorial insights.

"Dog"; Grace,
8 years old.

Introduction

When others ask me if I've always enjoyed humor, I immediately remember three different childhood scenarios. Each story illustrates that even as a kid, I valued the lighter side of life.

My first recollection is when I was 4 years old. Perched on a hammock in front of the brown plastic radio, I listened to the "Uncle Miltie Show." My parents encouraged me to tell his jokes to my grandfather. When I told the jokes with a great deal of 4-year-old spirit, everyone laughed. I learned very quickly that by telling jokes I could make people smile and feel more positive about life.

My second recollection is that my grandmother made sure that I went to a Catholic elementary school. The Sisters of Notre Dame ran the school. Although we were not Catholic, my parents thought I could learn discipline and structure from the good sisters. I survived to the sixth grade by being the class clown. As hard as the nuns tried to get me to conform—to see that their way was the right way—the more I thrived on the other kids' attention when we laughed and had fun together.

The third scene that I can clearly remember, after almost half a century, took place in seventh grade (after I broke away from the people who were trying to break my spirit). I decided that too many people walked around looking much too serious. I created a National Smile Day. I lived in Kansas City, but I had hopes of taking the day to a national level. I made badges, posters, and wrote a letter to the editor. At 12 years old, I thought I had the power to make the whole world smile. It is interesting to note that some calendars now recognize National Smile Day. I honestly don't believe the day has anything to do with my Smile Day. However, it is reassuring to know that someone actualized my seventh grade dream.

What began in my childhood grew throughout my life. My sense of humor and ability to laugh at myself enabled me to survive some very difficult situations growing up. It also helped me to survive living for years in an alcoholic marriage.

The older I grow (I'm not so old—I am wise before my time), the more I can see how the humorous and lighter part of me has been, and continues to be, a survival tool.

I recently passed my two-year mark battling cancer. I am convinced that a sense of humor is a necessary component for a healthy body, mind, and spirit. Research shows that there is a strong link between humor and health. I know that when I feel stressed from deadlines and other time crunches, my sense of humor is one of the first things that I put on the back burner. When I catch myself feeling too uptight, I look for cartoons and read stories in magazines and newspapers that make me smile. Some days the cartoons, stories, or jokes have to be very funny to break my tense mood.

"Dad"; Olivia, 4 years old.

In 1996, I took a risk and deviated from my traditional presentations. I began sharing stories about children and teachers that others passed on to me. The response was fantastic. People in the audience laughed, relaxed, and were able to thoroughly stay present with the topic of "Lighten Up and Live Longer." When I led the workshop for the first time at a national conference, Mary, the editor of this book, was walking down the hall headed to another session. She heard laughter coming out of one conference room. She went in to see why everyone was enjoying themselves so much. She soon joined me and 300 other workshop participants as we lightened up so we could live longer.

I also believe that balance is a component in a healthy lifestyle. Humor is part of that balance. When we feel stressed, we can restore balance by doing something relaxing. When we feel sad, we often cry. Even in the midst of sadness, we can find humor that can balance our emotions.

I decided to write this book because we have lives that are often filled with stress and intensity. Scientists, psychologists, holistic practitioners, traditional medical doctors, and our common sense tell us that to live longer we need to lighten up—to find relief from the tension in healthy ways. Developing and maintaining a healthy sense of humor is a tool for creating that balance in our lives. Most people appreciate a sense of humor.

"Blanket with a Sun" D.J., 6 years old.

People enjoy being around someone who balances the seriousness of life with humor.

In 1998, Robin Williams starred in the movie *Patch Adams*. Patch Adams became a doctor because he decided that humor was necessary for people's recovery. I totally agree with that philosophy. Did you know that when we belly-laugh our body releases endorphins, causing a biological reaction similar to the changes in a long distance runner's body? Isn't it wonderful to know that we can feel as good as someone who has been exercising strenuously, and we don't even have to break into a sweat?

I am fortunate to hear many stories about parents, children, grandparents, and teachers that help balance out the intensity of daily living. I collect e-mail messages from people all over the world that tell of humorous episodes involving people, animals, and work experiences.

This book is a collection of jokes, anecdotes, stories, and readings that I hope will bring a smile to your face and inspiration to your soul. This book is designed to bring some enjoyment into your life. Please don't read it all at one sitting. Pick it up. Read a little and laugh. And then put it down until the next time you want some fun or inspiration. As you read the book, you can share the thoughts and laughter with others—who can pass it on again. I hope that the world becomes a bit lighter and brighter because of this book's positive energy.

You will note that I have included blank pages at the end of each chapter so that you can add your own stories to this book. We are surrounded by humorous events and people daily. I hope this book will prompt you notice the joy and record your own jokes or stories. I hope you enjoy reading *Lighten Up and Live Longer.* I would love to hear your personal reaction.

You may contact me at:

2559 Hawthorne Lane, Stillwater, MN 55082-5266.
Phone and fax: 651-439-4100 or E-mail: baldwin@visi.com.
Website: www.suebaldwin.com

"Mom"; Alyse,
5½ years old.

"Two Friends"; Lauren, 9 years old.

Parents

I believe that most of us who are parents will agree that parenting is the most difficult job that we will ever have. I don't mean to discourage those of you who are parents of young children (or thinking of being parents), but this job never ends! No matter how old your child is, nothing grabs at your heart like a call late at night with a weepy voice on the other end, saying "Mom, I need to talk to you."

A sense of humor is a necessity in your parent survival toolbox. Something that may not seem very funny when it happens might bring a smile when you share the story later.

You might remember scribbles on the wall as your child's first attempt at creativity. I remember when my daughter Carrie was 3 years old. She dressed herself in a plaid skirt, striped tee-shirt and mismatched socks. When we went to church on Sundays I would repeat to myself (under my breath), "My child is not a reflection of me. She is her own person." I know we will repeat this story with much laughter when Carrie's children go through the same developmental stage.

I have found the best way to give advice to your children is to find out what they want and then advise them to do it.

HARRY TRUMAN

One way to keep your sense of humor is to develop friend-ships with other parents who have children around the same age as yours. You will find that once you start telling those friends stories about your children, they will share their own parenting tales. You will laugh with—not at—each other.

Laughter helps put a different slant on difficult situations. When our family had the flu and everyone was busy fending for themselves in the bathroom, it didn't seem very amusing. How-ever, when I told my friend our flu story, I realized that a miser-able situation can be humorous. The more she laughed, the less horrible the situation seemed.

Enjoy your children at whatever stage they are. Our minds do have a way of forgetting all of the horror stories. We learn how to appreciate what we have now in our lives.

What is my other advice to parents? Stay away from people who present their families as perfect. *Father Knows Best* is no longer in production. Laugh at yourself with your children and encourage them to develop a healthy sense of humor. Who knows? It could even be a lifesaver!

I hope that the stories in this chapter will help you laugh, be a better parent, or help someone who is a parent. Parenting can be tough work. These stories will put a different perspective on a difficult job. Whether you are a parent or not, I hope they bring smiles and balance into your life.

> *Kids learn more from example than anything you say. I'm convinced they learn very early not to hear anything you say, but to watch what you do.*
>
> JANE PAULEY

Family Dictionary

Feedback: The inevitable result when your baby doesn't appreciate the strained carrots.

Full name: What you call your children when you're mad at them.

Grandparents: The people who think your children are wonderful even though they're sure that you're not raising them right.

Hearsay: What toddlers do when anyone mutters a dirty word.

Amnesia: The condition that enables a woman who has gone through labor to make love again.

"A Girl"; Meeghan, 5 years old.

Dumbwaiter: One who asks if the kids would care to order dessert.

Impregnable: A woman whose memory of labor is still vivid.

Independent: How we want our children to be as long as they do everything we say.

Ow: The first word spoken by children with older siblings.

Puddle: A small body of water that draws other small bodies wearing dry shoes into it.

Showoff: A child who is more talented than yours.

Sterilize: What you do to your first baby's pacifier by boiling it and to your second baby's pacifier by blowing on it.

Top bunk: Where you should never put a child wearing Superman pajamas.

Two-minute warning: When your baby's face turns red and she begins to make those familiar grunting noises.

Verbal: Able to whine in words.

Whodunit: None of the kids who live in your house....

> *It's not easy to play the clown when you've got to run the whole circus.*
>
> HAWKEYE PIERCE IN *M*A*S*H*

Five-year-old Sara was mad at her dad for enforcing the rules.

Sara: "Dad, when I'm grown up and you're a child, you better watch out!"

> *If we allowed children to show us what they can do rather than merely accepting what they usually do, I feel certain we would be in for some grand surprises.*
>
> MEM FOX

Mom: (talking to her 2-year-old) "I love you to pieces, Natalie."
Natalie: "I love you all together!"

Three-year-old Luke saw a large scar on his mom's abdomen.
"What is that?" he asked.
"That's where the doctor cut open my belly to take you out," his mother replied.
Looking sad, Luke said, "Oh, Mama, I'm sorry I crawled in there."

Hanna's mom slid the cookie sheet into the oven.
Hanna said, "We'll know they're done when the smoke alarm goes off. Right, Mommy?"

> *Laughter is the shortest distance between two people.*
>
> VICTOR BORGE

Sophia was riding to a swimming class with her mom, who is a physician. Mom had left her stethoscope draped over the car seat. Sophia picked it up and began playing with it.

"Be still my heart," thought her mom. "My daughter wants to follow in my footsteps."

It wasn't long before Sophia spoke into the instrument. "Welcome to McDonald's. May I take your order?"

> *"If there is anything we wish to change in the child, we should first examine it and see whether it is not something that could be better changed in ourselves."*

C. J. Jung

Eight Things Parents Would Really Love

1. To have a family meal without a discussion about bodily secretions.
2. To be able to eat a whole candy bar alone.
3. To shower without a child peeking through the curtain with a "Hi ya!"
4. A full-time cleaning person who follows the children around, picking up messes.
5. Their teenager to announce, "I just got a full scholarship and a job all in the same day."
6. A grocery store that doesn't have candy, gum, and cheap toys displayed at the checkout line.
7. To be able to take their seats on a plane with a toddler and not have the person in front of them moan, "Oh, no! Why me?"

8. To have a teenager answer a question without rolling his eyes.

One day my 5-year-old daughter brought an art project home from child care. The word "CHRIST" was on the bottom corner. I was confused and concerned about this so the next morning I asked her teacher if she could tell me what happened. "Oh, Christine got tired of writing and didn't add the ending 'ine' to her name."

Our Opinion of Our Mother at :
4 Years Old: My mommy can do anything!
8 Years Old: My mom knows a lot! A whole lot!
12 Years Old: My mother doesn't know quite everything.
14 Years Old: Naturally, Mother doesn't know that, either.
16 Years Old: Mother? She's hopelessly old-fashioned.
18 Years Old: That old woman? She's way out of date!
25 Years Old: Well, she might know a little bit about some things.
35 Years Old: Before we decide, let's get Mom's opinion.
55 Years Old: I wonder if I should bother Mother with this when she isn't well.
75 Years Old: Wish I could talk it over with Mom.....

Mom: "I want to teach you about sex."
Child: "How can you teach me about sex? You have an 'F' after 'SEX' on your driver's license!"

Teacher: "Who can tell me why you love your mom."

Rebecca: "My mom fixes good food, takes us places, helps us, and she's the favorite wife of my dad!"

Nancy, mother of 3-year-old Lilly, normally wore slacks. But on Easter morning she came out of her bedroom in a dress. Lilly ran over to her, ran her hands up and down her mother's legs (mom was wearing nylons), wrapped her arms around mom's thighs, looked seriously up into her face, and said, "Mommy, are you a woman now?"

Four-year-old Dustin was in love with his child care teacher, Jennie. He asked his mom if he could ask his teacher to stay overnight at his house. Mom reminded him that Jennie had a house and a husband. Dustin looked at his mom with disgust in his eyes and said, "Well, I don't mean her whole family."

"Dad"; Maureen, 10 years old.

Phillip came home from his child care provider's house. His dad asked him to sing the song that Miss Carol had taught him that day. Phillip stood on the stairs and proudly belted out, "If you're happy with your nose—clap your hands!"

Tommy: "I can't wait until school tomorrow."

Mom: "That's great, Tommy. What are you most excited about—your new teacher, meeting new friends, or making art projects?"

Tommy: "I just can't wait to wear my new socks."

Two-and-a-half-year-old Katie was busy cleaning out the toilet bowl with a toothbrush.

Dad: "Katie, what are you doing cleaning out the toilet bowl with your toothbrush?"

"Toothbrush"; Tim, 30 years old

Katie: "It's not mine, Daddy. It's yours."

Three-year-old Henry had a runny nose, so his dad told him to go get a tissue. Henry stopped, sniffed, and said, "I don't need one. It just goes back in."

Nine-year-old Robert was working on a homework assignment and asked, "Dad, how do you spell VCR?"

One Sunday, Tyron, age 3, was having trouble sitting through the morning church service. His parents did their best to maintain some sense of order in the pew, but they were losing the battle. Finally, his father picked Tyron up and walked sternly up the aisle to leave the church. Just before they reached the foyer, Tyron called loudly to the congregation, "Pray for me! Pray for me!"

Dad listened to Courtney saying her prayers. When she said, "Dear Harold," her dad interrupted and asked, "Why do you call God Harold?"

Courtney looked up and said, "That's what they call Him in church. Yoooou know, we say, 'Our Father, who are in heaven, Harold be Thy name.'"

Four-year-old Erin was practicing her prayers. "And forgive us our trash baskets as we forgive those who put trash in our baskets," she prayed fervently.

Michael's parents overheard the 10-year-old saying his bedtime prayers:
"Now I lay me down to rest.
And hope to pass tomorrow's test.
But if I should die before I wake
That's one less test I'll have to take."

Ellie's mom invited some people to dinner. At the table she turned to her 6-year-old daughter and said, "Would you like to say the blessing?"

Ellie replied that she wouldn't know what to say. "Just say what you hear Mommy say," mom said.

Ellie bowed her head and said, "Dear Lord, why on earth did I invite all these people to dinner?"

A bright-colored mural of 8-year-old Lucas's favorite cartoon heroes decorated the upstairs hall wall. It was obviously drawn by a child with markers. Lucas's mom confronted him with the evidence.

"Wasn't me," Lucas said.

"Come on," Mom said. "Those are your markers on the floor and you're the only child in this house."

After more talking and tears, Lucas admitted he had lied.

Mom reminded Lucas, "You know that Mom doesn't always know when you are lying, but God always does."

Lucas quickly answered, "Yeah, but He doesn't always tell you."

Late Saturday night, 5-year-old Rachel's parents came to her room to kiss her goodnight. They had been out for dinner. Daddy had eaten an Italian dinner with all the trimmings. His breath smelled of garlic.

Sleepily, Rachel looked up from her dreams and asked, "Mommy, what am I made of?"

"Sugar and spice and everything nice, that's what little girls like you are made of," Mommy answered.

Rachel asked, "Oh. Then what are boys made of?"

Mommy answered, "Snips and snails and puppy dog tails, that's what boys are made of."

Pinching her eyebrows together and concentrating hard, Rachel looked at her daddy and said, "I guess that explains the smell!"

Three-year-old Olivia's mom, Traci, worked in the kitchen while Olivia played downstairs in the family room.

Traci called, "Olivia, what are you doing down there?"

Olivia answered proudly, "I'm making a mess, Mama."

Three-year-old Nick was talking to his new baby sister, Anna.

Nick (in a very high-pitched, soft voice): "Hi, baby sister."
Mom: "Nick, why do you talk that way to Anna?"
Nick: "Because I'm afraid my real Nick voice will scare her."

Three-year-old Ruby was trying to stop sucking her thumb. Mom gently reminded her that she had her thumb in her mouth. Ruby looked up at her mom with a big smile and said, "Sorry, Mommy. I thought it was a lollipop."

Four-year-old Georgia diligently pounded away on her father's word processor.
Georgia: "Daddy, I'm writing a story."
Daddy: "What is it about?"
Georgia: "I don't know. I can't read."

Kathy is telling her 8-year-old daughter, Rebecca, about her own childhood.
Kathy: "We used to skate outside on a pond. I had a swing made from a tire that hung on a tree in our front yard. We rode our pony. We picked wild raspberries in the woods."
Rebecca (wide-eyed, taking this all in): "I sure wish I'd gotten to know you sooner!"

After putting her children to bed, the twins' mother changed into old slacks and a droopy blouse. She began to wash her hair. She heard the children getting more and more rambunctious and her patience grew thin.
At last she threw a towel around her head and stormed into their room, putting them back to bed with a stern warning. As she left the room, she heard Richard say to Rachel in a trembling voice, "Who was that?"

"Mommy" Alexander, 4½ years old.

Five-year-old Simon said grace at the family dinner. "Dear God, thank you for these pancakes…" When he finished, his parents asked him why he thanked God for pancakes when they were having chicken. He smiled and said, "I thought I'd see if He was paying attention tonight."

On the ride back from the store, Christine was talking to her 6-year-old twins, Brady and Brian, about what they would do when they got home.

Christine said, "When we get home, I am going to do my exercise tape. I want you boys to go outside and play for 30 minutes."

With a puzzled look, Brady asked, "Mom, how come you exercise all the time, but you stay the same wide?"

The family finished watching a *National Geographic* program on television. The program showed animals mating. After many questions from both of her children, Judy knew that it was time to start talking to them about the facts of life.

Without being too graphic, Judy talked about the animals and then about what people did when they had sex.

Nine-year-old Jacob exclaimed with disgust, "You mean you did that two times?"

He thought for another minute and then said, "Oh no, Grandpa and Grandma must have done that four times?"

One afternoon at lunch, 3-year-old Michelle exclaimed, "Hey, there's a hot dog in my corn dog!"

My two daughters, Kris and Carrie, were trying to talk privately so my 3½-year-old grandson wouldn't partake in their conversation.

Kris: "Do you want to go to the F-I-R-E-W-O-R-K-S tonight?"

Carrie: "Sure, that would be great."

Nick (without knowing what was spelled): "Yeah, you can go with N-I-C-K."

"Mom and Dog"; Francesca, 5½ years old.

The Twelve Weeks of Summer

(sung to the tune of "The Twelve Days of Christmas")

12 Kids a-screaming
11 Weeks of "I'm bored!"
10 Headaches pounding
9 Million mosquitoes
8 Boxes of Band-Aids
7 Calamine bottles
6 Skateboard stitches
5 Ringing phones
4 Soccer tournaments
3 Hungry kids
2 Tired parents
1 Room at the sanatorium.

Nothing

When children come home at the end of the day
The question they're asked as they run out to play
Is "What did you today?"
And the answer they give makes you sigh with dismay
"Nothing. I did nothing today."
Perhaps nothing means that I played with blocks,
Or counted to ten, or sorted some rocks.
Maybe I painted a picture of red and blue,
Or heard a story of a mouse that flew.
Maybe I watched gerbils eat today,
Or went outside on the swings to play.
Maybe today was the very first time

That my scissors followed a very straight line.
Maybe I led a song from beginning to end,
Or played with a special brand-new friend.
When you're in preschool
And when your heart has wings,
"Nothing" can mean so many things!

Author unknown

Wet Oatmeal Kisses

One of these days you'll explode and shout to all the kids, "Why don't you just grow up and act your age!"

And they will.

Or, "You guys go outside and find something to do—without hurting each other. And don't slam the door!"

And they don't.

You'll straighten their bedrooms until they're all neat and tidy, toys displayed on the shelves, hangers in the closets, animals caged. You'll yell, "Now I want it to stay this way!"

And it will.

You will prepare a perfect dinner with a salad that hasn't had all the olives picked out and a cake with no finger traces in the icing and you'll say, "Now this is a meal for company."

And you will eat it alone.

You'll yell, "I want complete privacy on the phone. No screaming, do you hear me?"

And no one will answer.

No more plastic tablecloths stained. No more dandelion bouquets. No more iron-on patches. No more wet, knotted shoelaces, muddy boots, or rubber bands for ponytails.

Imagine...a lipstick with a point, no babysitters for New Year's Eve, washing clothes only once a week.

No PTA meetings or silly school plays where your child is a tree. No car pools, blaring stereos, or forgotten lunch money.

No more Christmas presents made of library paste and toothpicks. No wet oatmeal kisses, no more tooth fairy, no more giggles in the dark, no more scraped knees to kiss or sticky fingers to clean.

Only a voice asking, "Why don't you grow up?"

And the silence echos: "I did."

Author unknown

Marissa, 5 years old, was about to step into the bathtub.

Marissa: "I like it at the end of the day when I'm all dirty."

Mom: "Why is that?"

Marissa: "Because if I'm real dirty, that means I had a good day."

"Bath"; Vicki, 47 years old.

Your own stories

_____

_____

_____

_____

_____

_____

_____

_____

_____

_____

_____

_____

_____

_____

_____

_____

_____

_____

_____

_____

_____

_____

"Angel"; Olivia,
4 years old.

Teachers

You can be a teacher and lead a balanced life. Some days that may be hard to believe. Those are the days so full of stressful situations that we wonder why we ever chose this career. The stories in this chapter illustrate the delight that children bring to a teacher's world. When I asked teachers to share humorous incidents, most of them smiled and said "There are so many, I don't know where to begin."

It is children's naiveté and vulnerability that make them so innocent. Children see so many things through their fresh spirits. They constantly search for meaning and truth.

The relationship between teachers and children is special. When children are very young, the relationship is based on trust. Many times teachers are a child's first relationship with an adult outside their own family.

Children can express genuine love and caring to these professionals who touch their lives. When children trust their caregivers, they feel safe enough to say whatever is on their minds. That's why the stories from teachers are so precious. They reflect the trust that allows children to be free.

In turn, by being themselves, the children often make their teachers smile. I know how I feel when a parent tells me that their child talked about me all week. Or how excited their child was to come to see me. Comments like that bring out the joy in teaching and express the balance of the give and take of the profession.

No one teaches a child to be genuine, but they can welcome and honor the child's openness. In the following stories, we smile and laugh not at the children, but with them.

Whether you are a teacher or not, I hope that these stories will lift your spirits and bring a chuckle and even a few belly laughs into your world. Have you ever noticed how hard it is to be depressed around children when you really focus on their lives and spirits? Go ahead, forget your problems, let the kids help you lighten up and live longer. Enjoy!

※　※　※

Teacher: "Who has a happy thought that they would like to share with the class?"

Felicia: "I'm pregnant!"

Teacher: "I'm confused. Can you tell us more?"

Felicia: "Last night my mom said to my dad, 'Honey, I'm pregnant.' And he said, 'Now that's a happy thought.' "

Vicki was doing group time with her preschoolers. They were learning their addresses.

Olivia: "Miss Vicki, I don't know my ZIP code."

Tad: "Too bad. I know how to zip *my* coat."

> *What we learn from good teachers is how to teach ourselves better.*

JOHN HOLT

Cassandra sits with the toddlers at the lunch table. Jacob is eating a rice cake with peanut butter, so his tongue keeps getting stuck. The children are talking about some new toys in their room. Jacob tries unsuccessfully to add to the conversation. Cassandra looks at Jacob and says, "It's OK, Jacob, just spit it out."

Having been given permission, Jacob spits his rice cake out all over the other children.

"You're right teacher. Now I can talk."

> *You don't have to teach people to be funny. You only have to give them permission.*

DR. HARVEY MINDESS

The children in the prekindergarten room were learning their letters. It was "U" week. The teacher asked the children to name a word that started with "U."

When Becca's mom came to pick her up after school, Becca's teacher said, "It was so cute today when Becca used the word 'uterus' for her word during 'U' week."

Smiling and rolling her eyes, Mom responded, "Oh, yeah, great! And next week is 'V' week!"

It was noon on the first day of first grade. When the bell rang at noon, Ian went to get his backpack to go home.

Teacher: "Ian, first graders have lunch and stay all day at school."

Ian (looking exasperated): "Who in the heck signed me up for this?"

I hear and I forget. I see and I remember. I do and I understand.

CHINESE PROVERB

Knowledge is like a garden: If it is not cultivated, it cannot be harvested.

GUINEA PROVERB

Vicki was sitting on the floor with a small group of nursery school students. Ben came over and stood next to her.

Ben: "Miss Vicki, I have to go pee."

Vicki: "OK, Ben, you can go ahead and go."

Ben did exactly as he was told. He stood right there and peed on the floor.

> *People will pay more to be entertained than to be educated.*
>
> JOHNNY CARSON

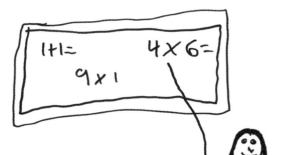

The children are making Mother's Day cards. Kelly, the teacher, spells out loud as she writes on Jordan's card. "To my mom—M-O-M," she says. Sallie pipes up, "That's how my mom spells her name!"

Amazed, three other children excitedly agree that their moms' names have the same spelling.

"Teacher"; Breane, 9 years old.

It was close to the holiday season. Lynn sat with a small group of children who were doing an art project. The children started talking about their Christmas trees at home.

Mark: "We have a great big star on the top of our tree."

Christopher: "We have a star with really bright lights on ours."

Anna: "We have lights that blink on the star on our tree."

Nicholas (looking rather dejected): "We just have a flying lady on ours."

The children were on a field trip to the local grocery store. The head of the meat department asked them if they knew where pork came from. Douglas proudly raised his hand and said, "A porcupine!"

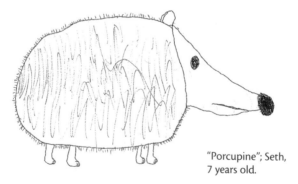

"Porcupine"; Seth, 7 years old.

It was popcorn day at kindergarten. The children talked about popcorn, pretended to be popcorn kernels, sang a popcorn song, popped corn, and made projects using popcorn.

Afterward, the teacher asked the children to tell her what they learned about popcorn. Paige said, "I learned that I don't like to eat popcorn with glue on it."

The children were walking down the hallway in their center. The door to the boys' bathroom was ajar. Tasha, a kindergartner, saw the urinal and said, "No fair! They get a drinking fountain in theirs!"

In the preschool room, they were reading "Bear Family Buys a Puppy." The story read, "So they picked out a puppy and Father Bear said, 'We want a boy puppy, so we'd better look under the tail and check.' " Savanah asked curiously, "Are their names written under their tails?"

During group time the children were talking about their siblings.
Jordan: "My brother takes horseback riding lessons."
Amanda: "My sister takes gymnastics."
Clara (not wanting to be outdone): "My sister takes antibiotics!"

The first graders at church were trying to learn the Lord's Prayer.
Grace: "I've got it....My father does artwork in heaven."

In the kindergarten class, Ashley had a student who brought some puppies from home to show her class.

Laura: "I can tell the girl puppies from the boy puppies. You pick them up, tip them over, and look at the bottoms of their feet."

"Cat"; Alisha, 9 years old.

The children in the Hebrew class were studying the Ten Commandments. They were ready to discuss the last one.

Teacher: "Can anyone tell me what the last commandment is?"

Noah: "Thou shall not take the covers off thy neighbor's wife."

The first grade class was brainstorming words that started with the letter "R."

Rahul said, "Rose."

"Like the flower?" his teacher asked.

"No." Raul replied, "Like Jesus Christ rose from the dead."

Jasper gave his first grade teacher some advice on having babies. "If you don't want to have more babies, you can always have your ribs tied," he said, knowingly.

Paul was having group time with his preschoolers. He said they were going to talk about the sounds that animals make.

Paul: "What sound does a cow make?"

Carter: "Moo."

Paul: "What sound does a rooster make?"

Luke: "Cock-a-doodle-do."

Paul: "What sound does a frog make?"

Danielle: "BUD!"

Paul: "I think you've been watching too many commercials on TV."

When the teacher asked Jessica if she had any brothers or sisters at home, Jessica replied, "No, I'm a lonely child."

Kim, a family child care provider, had 5-year-old Ryan at her home. As she was getting ready to lead their prayer before breakfast, Ryan interrupted her. He asked if he could say grace. Kim agreed. She grinned as Ryan ended his prayer with "...to the Father, the Son, and the Flowing Ghost!"

Madyson told her teacher about her kindergarten physical. "The doctor gave me one hug, and the nurse shot me twice."

Lydia, a kindergartner, was walking around the lake with her class. She noticed a large cluster of cattails by a swamp. "What are all those corn dogs doing out there sticking out of the water?" she asked.

Sandy, an assistant in the preschool room, was admiring Nora's beautiful red hair.

Sandy: "Nora, your hair is such a beautiful shade of red. Does everyone in your family have red hair?"

Nora: "Yes, except for my dad. He's a black head."

"Child with Chicken Pox" Alyson, 5 years old.

Ms. Olsen asked her kindergarten class if they had anything they wanted to talk about.

Cole said, "My brother, Trevor, has the chicken pox and he is turning into a Dalmatian!"

Rebecca, a 3-year-old in Patrick's preschool class, intently told a story about her kitty. She earnestly went into great detail.

As she finished, Patrick asked, "Rebecca, are you a serious person?"

Rebecca quickly responded, "No, silly. I'm a Catholic!"

Around the Christmas season, the children in the 4-year-old class discussed Santa Claus. They wondered at his magical ability to come down chimneys.

Remembering her fire safety lessons, Izabella explained to the others, "Santa comes down the chimney and then he stops, drops, and rolls."

I will not shout.
I will not push.
I will not throw things.
I will not have temper tantrums.
I AM THE TEACHER.

Eight Reasons to Become a Preschool Teacher
1. Cute little children...cute little paychecks.
2. Confidence that you will never, ever forget how to count to 10.
3. You get to sing your favorite songs over and over and over.
4. Play, play, play.
5. With all this bending, who needs aerobics?
6. Your classroom art is proudly displayed in many kitchen "galleries."
7. Small hands...large crayons.
8. You get to make little ones count.

Teacher: "Joshua, how is your bee sting?"
Joshua: "I had a bee-action." (reaction)

Forever In Your Heart
Although you're not their parent,
You care for them each day.
You cuddle, sing, and read to them
And watch them as they play.
You see each new accomplishment

You help them grow and learn
You understand their language
And you listen with concern.
They come to you for comfort
And you kiss away their tears.
They proudly show their work to you
You give the loudest cheers!
No, you are not their parent
But your role is just as strong.
You nurture them and keep them safe
Though maybe not for long.
You know someday the time will come
When you will have to part.
But you know each child you've cared for
Is forever in your heart!

Anonymous

> *Only positive consequences encourage good future performance.*
>
> KENNETH BLANCHARD AND ROBERT LORBER

> *A school should not be a preparation for life. A school should be life.*
>
> ELBERT HUBBARD

The third grade teacher was talking to the children about sex. She asked, "Children, what would you do if you found a condom on the porch?"

Joshua raised his hand and asked, "What's a porch?"

After an outbreak of chicken pox at school, Juanita asked the children if they ever had had the disease.

Samuel raised his hand and said, "No, but I've had fish sticks."

Partnership

They bring their child to me
And hope I'll come to know
How much their offspring means to them.
Their trust in me bestowed
They bring their child to me
With love, hope, and pride.
Looking for a helping hand,
A teacher who will guide.
They bring their child to me
And our partnership is clear.
To nurture and allow to bloom
A life we both hold dear.
They bring their child to me,
A step toward letting go
And trusting in our special plan
To help their child grow.

Anonymous

Your own stories

_____

_____

_____

_____

_____

_____

_____

_____

_____

_____

_____

_____

_____

_____

_____

_____

_____

_____

_____

_____

_____

_____

_____

_____

"Tornado"
Brad, 12 years old

Kids

Art Linkletter and Bill Cosby are two performers who hosted television shows with children. They asked children questions, the children responded, and the audience laughed at the children's answers. For decades we have found humor in the innocence of children.

As I stated in the introduction, when I was a child, I found that I received positive reinforcement for saying things that adults perceived as humorous. I wanted to include a chapter on kids in this book, because I believe that children's spontaneous responses and zest for life help contribute to an adult's ability to lighten up.

It is very difficult to be depressed around a 3-year-old. If we can focus on children and forget our problems for a while, children offer a balance to the intensity of adulthood. As I went through various treatments for cancer, I remembered that my young grandson could make me smile just by being himself. At the age of 1, he hadn't developed a sense of humor, but he gave me a reason for living. Nick lightened my stress with his presence. I distracted myself from pain and discomfort by focusing on the cute things he did.

I hope the following stories will help you lighten up and create balance in your life. Remember to fill in your own stories on the blank pages that you will find at the end of this chapter.

Four-year-old Adam was saying his prayers at bedtime. "Dear God, please take care of my daddy and my mommy and my sister and my brother and my doggy and me. Oh, please take care of yourself, God. If anything happens to you, we're going be in a big mess."

Carter was telling his friend Jason about the family's vacation in New York City and proudly explained that they got to go see the "Entire State Building."

> *We find delight in the beauty and happiness of children that makes the heart too big for the body.*
>
> RALPH WALDO EMERSON

Sadie, one of my grandson's 3-year-old friends, had dinner with her parents at a restaurant. They served fortune cookies at the end of the meal. Sadie's parents read their fortunes aloud. Her father offered to read Sadie's. Sadie, wanting to use her independence skills, said, "I'll read this myself. It says 'You are going to get a fortune cookie for dessert.' "

Matthew and Michelle were playing outside in the sandbox. Michelle: "I'll bet you don't know what a honeymoon is." Matthew: "Uh huh, that's when two people get married, go on a plane, go to Hawaii, eat pineapples, and get pregnant."

Do you know the difference between Brussels sprouts and boogers? Kids won't eat Brussels sprouts.

Toddlers' Property Laws
If I like it—it's mine.
If it's in my hand—it's mine.
If I can take it from you—it's mine.
If I had it a little while ago—it's mine.
If it's mine, it must never appear to be yours in any way.
If I'm doing or building something—all the pieces are mine.
If it looks like mine—it's mine.

Author unknown

Children are a wonderful gift. They have an extraordinary capacity to see into the heart of things and to expose sham and humbug for what they are.

ARCHBISH DESMOND TUTU

You know you're a child of the 90s when...
You've always called people on the phone using 10 digits.
You don't know what a typewriter is.
Your first dance steps were the "Macarena."
You use the Internet more than you use the telephone.
You've always had to pass through a metal detector to go to school.
Your name is Ashley or Jordan.

Question: Do you know what a toddler and a tornado have in common? Answer: They can both destroy a house in a matter of minutes.

David was leaving the store with his mom. When an elderly gentleman held the door open for them David said, "Thank you." "Don't mention it," replied the man. "But Mama told me to," David said.

Quotes from 11-year-olds' Science Exam:

■ Water is composed of two kinds of gin: oxy-gin and hydro-gin. Oxygen is pure gin, and hydrogen is gin and water.
■ When you breathe, you inspire; when you do not breathe, you expire.
■ H_2O is hot water, and CO_2 is cold water.
■ Three kinds of blood vessels are arteries, veins, and caterpillars.
■ To keep milk from turning sour, keep it in the cow.
■ To prevent contraception, wear a condominium.
■ Equator: A menagerie lion running around the Earth through Africa.
■ Dew is formed on leaves when the sun shines down on them and makes them perspire.
■ Vacuum: A large, empty space where the pope lives.

A rabbi said to precocious 6-year-old Sarah, "So your mother says your prayers for you each night. How commendable.

What does she say?" Sarah looked up at the elder man and said, "Thank God she's in bed."

Quotes About Kids

Children are remarkable for their intelligence and ardor, for their curiosity, their intolerance of shams, and the clarity and ruthlessness of their vision.

ALDOUS HUXLEY

Pretty much all the honest truth-telling there is in the world is done by children.

OSCAR WILDE

Even a minor event in the life of a child is an event of that child's world, and thus a world event.

GASTON BACHELARD

You know children are growing up when they start asking questions that have answers.

JOHN J. PLOMP

Children in a family are like flowers in a bouquet. There's always one determined to face in an opposite direction from the way the arranger desires.

MADELINE COX

Children are likely to live up to what you believe of them.

LADY BIRD JOHNSON

Children are like puppies; you have to keep them near you and look after them if you want their affection.

ANNA MAGNANI

Every baby born into the world is a finer one than the last.

CHARLES DICKENS

Babies are such a nice way to start people.

DON HEROLD

Great Truths about Life that Little Children Know

1. No matter how hard you try, you cannot baptize cats.
2. When your mom is mad at your dad, don't let her brush your hair.
3. If your sister hits you, don't hit her back. They always catch the second person.
4. Never ask your 3-year-old brother to hold a tomato.
5. You can't trust dogs to watch your food.
6. Don't sneeze when someone is cutting your hair.

7. Puppies still have bad breath after eating a Tic Tac.
8. Never hold a Dustbuster and a cat at the same time.
9. School lunches stick to the wall.
10. Don't wear polka-dot underwear under white shorts.
11. The best place to be when you are sad is on Grandma's lap.

"Polka Dots"
Roxanne, 56 years old.

How to Really Love a Child

Be there. Say "YES" as often as possible. Let them bang on pots and pans. If they're crabby, put them in water. If they're unlovable, love yourself. Realize how important it is to be a child. Go to a movie theater in your pajamas. Read books out loud with joy. Invent pleasures together. Remember how really small they are. Giggle a lot. Surprise them. Say "NO" when necessary. Teach feelings. Heal your own inner child. Learn about parenting. Hug trees together. Make loving safe. Bake a cake and eat it with no hands. Go find elephants and kiss them. Plan to build a rocket ship. Imagine yourself magic. Make lots of forts with blankets. Let your angel fly. Reveal your own dreams. Search out the positive. Keep the gleam in your eye. Mail letters to God. Encourage silly. Plant licorice in your garden. Open up. Stop yelling. Express your love. A lot. Speak kindly. Paint their tennis shoes. Handle with care. Remember: Children Are Miraculous.

Anonymous

Fifth Grade Proverbs

A fifth-grade-teacher collected well-known proverbs. She gave each child in her class the first half of a proverb and asked them to complete it. Here is what they had to say:

Better to be safe than...punch a fifth grader.

Strike while the...bug is close.

It's always darkest before...Daylight Savings Time.

Never underestimate the power of...termites.

You can lead a horse to water, but...how?

Don't bite the hand that...looks dirty.

No news is...impossible.

You can't teach an old dog...new math.

If you lie down with dogs, you'll...stink in the morning.

The pen is mightier than...the pigs.

An idle mind is...the best way to relax.

Where there is smoke, there is...pollution.

Happy is the bride who...gets all the presents.

A penny saved is...not much.

Two's company, three's...the Musketeers.

Don't put off 'til tomorrow what...you put on to go to bed.

Laugh and the whole world laughs with you; cry and...you have to blow your nose.

Children should been seen and not...spanked or grounded.

If at first you don't succeed...get new batteries.

You get out of something what you...see pictured on the box.

> *Childhood is frequently a solemn business for those inside it.*
>
> GEORGE WILL

The Things Kids Say to God

Dear God, Instead of letting people die and having to make new ones, why don't You just keep the ones You have? *Jane*

Dear God, Maybe Cain and Abel would not kill each other so much if they had their own rooms. It works with my brother. *Larry*

Dear God, If You watch me in church on Sunday, I'll show You my new shoes. *Mickey*

Dear God, I bet it is very hard for You to love everybody in the whole world. There are only four people in our family and I can never do it. *Nan*

Dear God, In school they told us what You do. Who does it when You are on vacation? *Jane*

Dear God, I read the Bible. What does "begot" mean? Nobody will tell me. Love, *Allison*

"A Dog"
Nicole, 5 years old.

Dear God, Thank you for the baby brother, but what I prayed for was a puppy. *Joyce*

Dear God, Are You really invisible or is it just a trick? *Lucy*

Dear God, Is it true my father won't get into heaven if he uses his bowling words in the house? *Anita*

"Giraffe"
Joe, 27 years old

Dear God, Did You mean for the giraffe to look like that or was it an accident? *Norma*

Dear God, Who draws the lines around the countries? *Nan*

Dear God, Did You really mean "Do unto others as they do unto you"? Because if You did, then I'm going to fix my brother. *Darla*

Dear God, Why is Sunday school on Sunday? I thought it was supposed to be our day of rest. *Tom*

Dear God, Please send me a pony. I never asked for anything before. You can look it up. *Bruce*

Dear God, If we come back as something, please don't let me be Mary Horton because I hate her. *Denise*

Dear God, If you give me a genie like Aladdin, I will give You anything You want, except my money or my chess set. *Raphael*

Dear God, I want to be just like my daddy when I get big but not with so much hair all over. *Sam*

Dear God, You don't have to worry about me. I always look both ways. *Dean*

Dear God, I think about You sometimes even when I'm not praying. *Elliott*

Dear God, My brother told me about being born but it doesn't sound right. He's just kidding, isn't he? *Marsha*

Dear God, We read that Thomas Edison made light. But in Sunday school they said You did it. So I bet he stole your idea. *Donna*

Dear God, I do not think anybody could be a better God. And I want You to know, but I am not just saying that because You are God already. *Charles*

Dear God, I didn't think orange went with purple until I saw the sunset You made on Tuesday. That was cool. *Eugene*

Dear God, I think the stapler is one of your greatest inventions. *Ruth*

Your own stories

_____

_____

_____

_____

_____

_____

_____

_____

_____

_____

_____

_____

_____

_____

_____

_____

_____

_____

_____

_____

_____

_____

_____

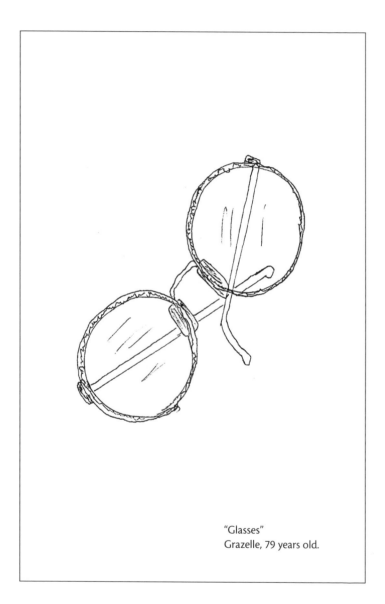

"Glasses"
Grazelle, 79 years old.

Bits and Pieces

When I think about this chapter, I think about the famous junk drawer that most of us have in our kitchens. We have very important things in there: matchbooks, rubber bands, coins, loose batteries, etc. In our junk drawers we know where to find certain things that don't seem to have a special place within our other, more organized drawers. And so it is with this chapter. You will find jokes, anecdotes, and stories that don't have a place within the other chapters of this book. I hope you will once again decide to fill up the blank pages at the end of this chapter with bits and pieces of humor that you want to keep for years to come.

> *If you think you're too small to have an impact, try going to bed with a mosquito.*
>
> ANITA KODDICK

> *He who cannot dance will say, "The drum is bad."*
>
> ASHANTI PROVERB

Think About It

Clones are people two.

Go ahead and take risks. Just be sure that everything will turn out okay.

If you can't be kind, at least have the decency to be vague.

Ever wonder what the speed of lightning would be if it didn't zigzag?

Think "honk" if you're telepathic.

If a cow laughs, does milk come out of her nose?

I went for a walk last night and my kids asked me how long I'd be gone. I said, "The whole time."

So what is the speed of dark?

After eating, do amphibians need to wait an hour before getting out of the water?

Why don't they just make mouse-flavored cat food?

If you're sending someone some Styrofoam, what do you pack it in?

I just got skylights put in my place. The people who live above me are furious.

Isn't Disney World a people trap operated by a mouse?

How come "abbreviated" is such a long word?

If it's zero degrees outside today and it's supposed to be twice as cold tomorrow, how cold is it going to be?

"Cat"
Devin, 9 ½ years old.

I believe you should live each day as if it is your last, which is why I don't have any clean laundry because, come on, who wants to wash clothes on the last day of their life?

Bumper Stickers
A day without sunshine is called night.
Honk if you love peace and quiet.
Despite the high cost of living, have you noticed how popular it remains?
Depression is merely anger without enthusiasm.
Borrow money from pessimists—they don't expect it back.
Experience is something you don't get until just after you need it.

It sure would be nice if we got a day off for the president's birthday, like the English do for the queen's birthday. Of course, then we would have a lot of people voting for a candidate born on July 3 or December 26 just to get a long weekend.

Did You Know?
1. Kotex was first manufactured as bandages during World War I.
2. Einstein couldn't speak fluently when he was nine. His parents thought that he might be retarded.
3. In Los Angeles, there are fewer people than automobiles.
4. About one-third of all Americans flush the toilet while they're sitting on it.

5. You're more likely to get stung by a bee on a windy day than in any other weather.
6. The average person laughs 15 times a day.
7. Research indicates that mosquitoes are attracted to people who have just eaten bananas.
8. Penguins can jump as high as six feet in the air.
9. The average person is one-half-inch taller upon rising in the morning than she was when she went to bed.
10. A sneeze zooms out of your mouth at 600 mph.
11. Thomas Edison was afraid of the dark.
12. Every person has a unique tongue print.
13. Your right lung takes in more air than your left lung does.
14. Women's hearts beat faster than men's hearts.
15. Pollsters say that 40 percent of dog and cat owners carry pictures of their pets in their wallets.
16. You can smell only 1/20th as well as a dog can.
17. In the movie E.T., the sound of E.T. walking was made by someone squishing her hands in Jell-o.
18. If you cut off a cockroach's head, the head can live for weeks.
19. Most American car horns honk in the key of F.
20. Every time Beethoven sat down to write music, he poured ice water over his head.
21. In 75 percent of American households, women manage the money and pay the bills.
22. Sigmund Freud had an intense fear of ferns.
23. Mosquitoes have teeth.
24. Spotted skunks do handstands before they spray.
25. When snakes are born with two heads, they fight each other for food.

Death is nature's way of telling us to slow down.

ANONYMOUS

Three to five minutes of intense laughter (or 100 belly laughs) can double your heart rate. This is the aerobic equivalent of three strenuous minutes on a rowing machine.

DR. WILLIAM FRY

The Difference between an Acquaintance and a Real Friend

Anyone can stand by you when you are right, but a friend will stand by you even when you are wrong.

An acquaintance identifies himself when he calls. A real friend doesn't have to.

An acquaintance opens a conversation with a full news bulletin about her life. A real friend says, "What's new with you?"

An acquaintance thinks the problems you whine about are recent. A real friend says, "You've been whining about the same thing for 14 years. Get off your duff and do something about it."

An acquaintance has never seen you cry. A real friend has shoulders soggy from your tears.

An acquaintance doesn't know your parents' first names. A real friend has their phone numbers in her address book.

An acquaintance brings a bottle of wine to your party. A real friend comes early to help you cook and stays late to help you clean.

An acquaintance hates it when you call after she goes to bed. A real friend asks you why you took so long to call.

An acquaintance seeks to talk with you about your problems. A real friend seeks to help you with your problems.

An acquaintance wonders about your romantic history. A real friend could blackmail you with it.

An acquaintance, when visiting, acts like a guest. A real friend opens your refrigerator and helps herself.

An acquaintance thinks the friendship is over when you have an argument. A real friend knows that it's not a friendship until after you've had a fight.

An acquaintance expects you to always be there for her. A real friend expects to always be there for you!

The Shape Women are In
Did you know ....

If shop mannequins were real women, they'd be too thin to menstruate.

There are three billion women who don't look like supermodels and only eight women who do.

Marilyn Monroe wore a size 16.

If Barbie were a real woman, she'd have to walk on all fours because of the way she's proportioned.

The average American woman weighs 144 pounds and wears between size 12 and 14.

One out of every four college-aged women has an eating disorder.

The models in the magazines are airbrushed. They're not really perfect!

A psychological study in 1995 found that three minutes spent looking at models in a fashion magazine caused 70 percent of women to feel depressed, guilty, and ashamed.

Twenty years ago, models weighed 8 percent less than the average woman. Today, models weigh 23 percent less than the average woman.

The need for change bulldozed a road down the center of my mind.

MAYA ANGELOU

When people keep telling you that you can't do a thing, you kind of like to try it.

MARGARET CHASE SMITH

Questions to Ponder

When someone asks you, "A penny for your thoughts," and you put in your two cents worth, what happens to the other penny?

When cheese gets its picture taken, what does it say?

Do Roman paramedics refer to IVs as "4s?"

Why is it that if someone tells you that there are one billion stars in the universe you will believe them, but if they tell you a wall has wet paint you have to touch it to be sure?

A bus station is where a bus stops. A train station is where a train stops. On my desk, I have a work station.

If FedEx and UPS were to merge, would they call it FedUp?

STRESSED spelled backwards is DESSERTS.

Nostalgia isn't what it used to be.

> *Some people look upon any setback as the end. They are always looking for the benediction rather than the invocation.*
>
> HUBERT HUMPHREY

> *Truly great people emit a light that warms the hearts of those around them*
>
> BANANA YOSHIMOTO

Girl to Woman

You were born a daughter.
You looked up to your mother.
You looked up to your father.
You looked up to everyone.
You wanted to be a princess.
You wanted to own a horse.
You wanted your brother to be a horse.
You wanted to wear pink.
You *never* wanted to wear pink.
You wanted to be a veterinarian.
You wanted to be president.
You wanted to be the president's veterinarian.
You were picked last for the team.
You were the best one on the team.
You refused to be on the team.
You wanted to do well in algebra.
You hid during algebra.
You wanted boys to notice you.
You were afraid the boys would notice you.

"Girl"
Kelly, 8 years old.

You didn't care if the boys noticed you.
You started to get acne.
You started to get breasts.
You started to get acne that was bigger than your breasts.
You couldn't wait to wear a bra.
You wouldn't wear a bra.
You didn't like the way you looked.
You didn't like the way your parents looked.
You couldn't wait to grow up.
You didn't want to grow up.
You had your first best friend.
You had your first date.
You spent hours on the telephone.
You got kissed.
You got to kiss back.
You didn't go to the prom.
You went to the prom.
You went to the prom with the wrong person.
You spent hours on the telephone.
You fell in love.
You fell in love.
You fell in love.
You lost your best friend.
You lost your other best friend.
You really fell in love.
You became a steady girlfriend.
You became a significant other.
You learned how to be a best friend again.
You became significant to yourself.
You start to take yourself seriously.

You know when you need a break.
You know when you need a rest.
You know what to get worked up about and what to get rid of.
You know when it's time to take care of yourself, to do something that makes you stronger, faster, and more complete.
You know it's never too late to live life—
And never too late to change one.

Anonymous

For centuries, people thought the moon was made of green cheese. Then the astronauts found that the moon is really a big hard rock. Shows what happens to cheese when you leave it out.

Normal is only a cycle on a washing machine.

Actual Classified Ads Bloopers

AMANA WASHER $100—OWNED BY A CLEAN BACHELOR WHO SELDOM WASHED.

SNOW BLOWER FOR SALE—USED ONLY ON SNOWY DAYS.

FREE: YORKSHIRE TERRIER. 8 YEARS OLD. UNPLEASANT LITTLE DOG.

AMERICAN FLAG—60 STARS. POLE INCLUDED—$100.

GEORGIA PEACHES—CALIFORNIA GROWN—89 CENTS A POUND

NICE PARACHUTE: NEVER OPENED—USED ONCE—SLIGHTLY STAINED.

A perfectly normal person is rare in our civilization.

KAREN HORNEY

To know is nothing at all; to imagine is everything.

ANATOLE FRANCE

Life is too serious to be taken seriously.

OSCAR WILDE

I bet living in a nudist colony takes all the fun out of Halloween.

"Kitty Cat"
Emma,
4 years old.

Your own stories

_____

_____

_____

_____

_____

_____

_____

_____

_____

_____

_____

_____

_____

_____

_____

_____

_____

_____

_____

_____

_____

_____

_____

"Grandma"
Grace, 8 years old.

Grandparents

I will never forget a Mother's Day not long ago. My daughter Kris and her husband, Tim, gave me a book called *Our Granny,* by Margaret Wild (New York, NY: Picknor & Fields Books, 1994). A handwritten message on the inside cover informed me that before Christmas, I would become a grandparent for the first time. I cried with happiness, as did Kris and Tim. What a wonderful gift!

I loved seeing Kris grow throughout her pregnancy. Kris and Tim invited me to participate in Nicholas' birth. Tim stood at the head of the bed encouraging Kris. I helped her pull her knees to her forehead. Seeing Nick's little body pop out was the most wonderful sight in the world.

Three years later, Anna was born. This time Tim moved to the catching position. I stayed close by Kris and coached and whispered words of encouragement to her. I became a grandparent for the second time.

Grandparenting makes parenting all worthwhile. I believe that parenting is the hardest job anyone will ever have. Being a grandparent is a very special gift that rewards parents for raising their own children.

I have always been one of those people who could hardly wait to become a grandparent. I know that grandparenting is another opportunity to be a special part of someone's life. Grandparents get a second chance to do things right. Also, most of us can send the grandchildren home after a relatively brief visit. Then we can rest and regroup for the next time. Some grandparents are raising their grandchildren. I give them a great deal of credit for taking on the total parenting role all over again.

I become totally absorbed when I play with my grandchildren. All of my professional responsibilities seem unimportant. I am busy playing cars, building sand castles, or blowing bubbles in the wind. Writing proposals or balancing a budget are not as important as teaching a young child how to skip, plant a flower, or jump off the diving board.

Some of my friends do not have grandchildren. So I share! My grandchildren give each of these friends a special name. The lucky friends play an important role in each of my grandchildren's circle of grownup friends.

Other grandparents shared many of the cute stories in this chapter. I really wanted to fill many pages with stories from and about my grandchildren. But I had to admit that there are many other grandparents with great stories, too! These stories are real treasures that I am honored to share—along with stories about my grandkids, of course!

Many children have special relationships with their grandparents. The tension that can occur between parents and children often does not exist between grandparents and children. There are tons of unconditional love going in both directions. That is probably why, no matter how old we are, we cherish our happy memories of our grandparents.

In group time, the teacher was talking to the children about their grandparents.

Teacher: "Jack, what is your grandpa's name?"

Jack: "His name is Bert."

Lisa: "Does that mean your grandma's name is Ernie?"

Five-year-old Ronnie called his grandma to tell her that he had to get glasses.

Grandma: "Are you nearsighted or farsighted?"

Ronny: "I am REAL excited, Grandma."

As Erika and Grandpa rode in the car, she gave him an anatomy lesson.

Erika: "I have two eyes, two ears, two arms, two legs, two elbows, and two knees."

Grandpa: "I have four knees. A right knee, a left knee, and two kidneys."

Erika (without skipping a beat): "No, Grandpa, I have kid knees. You have grandpa knees."

> *Treat people as if they were what they ought to be, and you help them to become what they are capable of being.*
>
> JOHANN WOLFGANG VON GOETHE

Emily was at a restaurant with her grandpa. He ordered, "Eggs, easy on the salt, please." She had heard her grandpa do this several times.

The next time they ate breakfast out, the server asked Emily what she wanted to drink. Emily responded, "Hot chocolate. Easy on the hot, please."

Bradley: "My grandpa has a whole drawer full of candy."
Tad: "Well, my grandpa has that, too."
Bradley: "Yeah, but this one you can reach."

Kristin, age 4, was in a very finicky mood and refused to eat any of her dinner. Her mother explained that it was important to eat Mommy's cooking because food would give her energy. Kristin ate her dinner. Later, in a telephone conversation with her grandmother, Kristin proudly announced, "Mommy's cooking gives me injuries!"

Hannah decided to scare her grandson a few days before Halloween by dressing up as a witch. It was the middle of the day and she hid in the woods waiting for him to pass by with his buddy. Hannah went to extreme measures—a wig, face painted green, different shoes—so that he would not recognize her.

When Zack and his friend got close she jumped out in front of them but didn't say anything because she didn't want him to recognize her voice.

Zack looked at Hannah and said, "Grandma, what are you doing here?"

"Grandma"
Karen, 45 years old.

Quotes about Grandparenting

The secret to a happy life is to skip having children and go directly to the grandchildren.

MOMMA (A CARTOON CHARACTER
CREATED BY MEL LAZARUS)

Perfect love sometimes does not come until the first grandchild.

WELSH PROVERB

If nothing is going well, call your grandmother or grandfather.

ITALIAN PROVERB

Your sons weren't made to like you. That's what grandchildren are for.

JANE SMILEY

A grandmother is a baby-sitter who watches the kids instead of the television.

ANONYMOUS

Our grandchildren accept us for ourselves, without rebuke or effort to change us, as no one in our entire lives has ever done. Not our parents, siblings, spouses, friends—and hardly ever our own grown children.

RUTH GOODE

Dearer than our children are the children of our children.

EGYPTIAN PROVERB

Children's children are a crown to the aged, and parents are the pride of their children.

PROVERBS 17:6

Children have never been very good at listening to their elders, but they have never failed to imitate them.

JAMES BALDWIN

The closest friends I have made all through life have been people who also grew up close to a loved and loving grandmother and grandfather.

MARGARET MEAD

If you would civilize a man, begin with his grandmother.

VICTOR HUGO

What's so simple even a small child can manipulate it? Why, a grandmother, of course!

ANONYMOUS

It is as grandmothers that our mothers come into the fullness of their grace. When a man's mother holds his child in her gladden arms he is aware of the roundness of life's cycle, of the mystic harmony of life's ways.

CHRISTOPHER MORLEY

No cowgirl was ever faster on the draw than a grandma pulling baby pictures out of her handbag.

ANONYMOUS

You often meet grandparents who bore you about their grandchildren, but never vice versa.

ANONYMOUS

Some people make the world more special just by being in it.

ANONYMOUS

Grandma heard Noah saying his prayers before bedtime.

"Lord, if You can't make me a better boy, don't worry about it. I'm having a real good time like I am!"

At Christmas time, 3-year-old Edward put a small toy jeep into the manger scene. Grandpa asked him why he did that. Edward replied, "So Joseph can get his family around a little easier."

Four-year-old Katie sat on her grandpa's lap. She started playing with his mustache.

Katie: "What is this fur on your face, Grandpa?"

Grandpa: "That's called a mustache."

Katie: "A mud stash?"

Justin: "Grandma, do you know how you and God are alike?"

Grandma (mentally polishing her halo): "No, how are we alike?"

Justin: "You're both old."

"Mud Stash"
David, 60 years old.

Grandpa had been working with 10-year-old Ross on his Sunday school assignment.

Ross asked, "Grandpa, which virgin was the mother of Jesus—the Virgin Mary or the King James Virgin?"

Patrick: "Grandma, will you play tag with us?"
Grandma: "Oh, no honey. I am too old."
Patrick: "Grandma, you are really old, but you aren't an antique yet!"

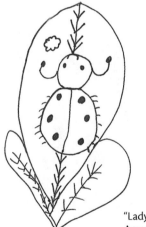

"Ladybug"
Amanda, 7 years old.

Ruth affectionately called her granddaughters "ladybugs" from the time they were born.

When Amanda was 7 years old, she asked, "Grandma, why do you call us 'ladybugs?' Is it because we bug you?"

Ruth smiled, thinking that was a very good reason.

"Shmily"

My grandparents were married for over half a century. They played their own special game from the time they met each other. The goal of their game was to write the word "shmily" in a surprise place for the other to find.

They took turns leaving "shmily" around the house. As soon as the other person discovered it, the other partner took their turn to hide it once more.

They dragged "shmily" with their fingers through the sugar and flour containers, to await whoever was preparing the next meal. They smeared it in the dew on the windows overlooking the patio (where Grandma always fed us warm, homemade pudding with blue food coloring).

They wrote "shmily" in the steam left on the mirror after a hot shower, where it would reappear bath after bath. At one point, my grandma even unfurled an entire roll of toilet paper, to leave "shmily" on the very last sheet. There was no end to the places "shmily" would pop up. Little notes with "shmily" scribbled hurriedly were found on dashboards and car seats, or taped to steering wheels.

Grandma and Grandpa stuffed notes inside shoes and left them under pillows. "Shmily" appeared in the dust

"Grandma"
Lauren, 9 years old.

upon the mantel and traced in the ashes of the fireplace. This mysterious word was as much a part of my grandparents' house as the furniture.

It took me a long time before I was able to fully appreciate my grandparents' game. Skepticism kept me from believing in true love—one that is pure and enduring—except in my grandparents' relationship. They had love down pat.

"Grandpa"
Breane,
9 years old.

It was more than their flirtatious little games. It was a way of life. Their relationship was based on devotion and passionate affection—attributes that not everyone is lucky enough to experience.

Grandma and Grandpa held hands every chance they could. They stole kisses as they bumped into each other in their tiny kitchen. They finished each other's sentences and shared the daily crossword puzzle and word jumble.

My grandma whispered to me about how cute my grandpa was, how much even more handsome he had grown to be. She claimed that she "really knew how to pick 'em."

Before every meal my grandparents bowed their heads and gave thanks. They marveled at their blessings: a wonderful family, good fortune, and each other.

One day, suddenly it seemed, a dark cloud cast a shadow on my grandparents' lives. My grandma's breast cancer, gone for 10 years, reappeared.

As always, Grandpa was with her every step of the way. He comforted her in their yellow room. He painted it that color so that Grandma could always be surrounded by sunshine even when she was too sick to go outside.

This time the cancer attacked her entire body. Even then, with the help of a cane and my grandpa's steady hand, they went to church every morning. My grandma grew steadily weaker. Finally, she could not leave the house anymore. For a while, Grandpa would go to church alone, praying to God to watch over his wife.

One day, as he prayed in church, my beloved grandma left the earth.

At the wake, "shmily" was scrawled in yellow on the pink ribbons of my grandma's funeral bouquet. As the crowd thinned and the last mourners turned to leave, my aunts, uncles, cousins, and other family members came forward and gathered around Grandma one last time. Grandpa stepped up to my grandma's casket. Taking a shaky breath, he began to sing to her.

Through his tears and grief, he crooned a deep-throated lullaby. Shaking with my own sorrow, I knew that I would never forget that moment.

"S-h-m-i-l-y," he sang, each letter coming out crisply despite his sadness. "Put them all together they spell 'shmily'. **S**ee **h**ow **m**uch **I** **l**ove **y**ou. See how much I love you. Every day. In every way."

We finally knew what their secret word meant.

We cried more, honored to witness the unmatched beauty of their love. As Grandpa bent over the casket to give Grandma her final kiss, we all sang softly, "Shmily. See how much I love you. See how much I love you. Every day. In every way."

Anonymous

Lyssa: "Grandma, you smell so good. Is that Oil of Old Lady?"

Six-year-old Jessica visited her grandparents' house. To help her with her spelling, Grandma asked her how to spell various words. Jessica spelled them all correctly.

With a twinkle in her eye, Grandma said, "Now I am going to give you a hard one. Can you spell 'Mother'?"

"M-O-M-M-Y!" Jessica replied, with a matching twinkle.

Jacob: "Grandpa, can you make the sound of a frog?"

Grandpa: "Why do you want me to do that?"

Jacob: "Because Dad says that when you croak, we're going to be rich."

"Frog"
Libby, 9 years old.

My 3-year-old grandson, Nick, was leaving my house. I remembered that we hadn't done our good-bye rituals. So I asked, "Nick, can I have a hug today?"

Nick answered, "No, Nana, no hug today."

Sounding rejected, I asked, "Then can I have a kiss?"

"No, Nana," Nick replied, "I'm not giving kisses today."

Sounding desperate, I asked, "Then what can I have?"

Smiling a smug 3-year-old smile, Nick said, "You can just have a 'Bye!'"

> *No matter how full the river, it still wants to grow.*
>
> CONGO PROVERB

Grandma had Victoria over for lunch and asked her what she wanted to eat. "Chicken soup," she answered.

Grandpa was working in the garden. Knowing that Grandpa wouldn't eat soup, Grandma went outside and asked him what he wanted. "Just give me a can of sardines," said Grandpa.

When they all sat down to eat lunch together, Victoria looked puzzled and asked, "Why is Grandpa eating cat food?"

"Sardines"
Roxanne, 56 years old.

My grandmother started walking five miles a day when she was 60 years old. She's 97 now and we don't know where in the heck she is.

It was sharing time at preschool. Dustin brought out pictures of three grandmas.

Teacher: "Is one of these a great-grandma?"

Dustin: "No, they're all good grandmas."

Your own stories

_____

_____

_____

_____

_____

_____

_____

_____

_____

_____

_____

_____

_____

_____

_____

_____

_____

_____

_____

_____

_____

"Girl"
Heather, 9 years old.

Free Advice

I have a personal philosophy about advice. I usually don't like to give it. When people ask me for my advice, I usually encourage them to find the answer within themselves. That is one of the many counseling techniques I learned in college.

However, this chapter is filled with free advice that was neither solicited by you, nor is it something that I think you wouldn't be able to live without. I do believe that you will have fun with many of these ideas and perhaps they will help you lighten up just a little.

❋　❋　❋

If people could only concentrate on their strengths as wholeheartedly as they concentrate on their weaknesses, success would be assured.

Spiders, snakes, bats, and negative people do one thing: they give people the creeps!

Each person has a mental picture of an ideal self. Moving toward that mental picture is what makes people feel good about themselves. It's not what we think we are that holds us back; it's what we think we are not.

Very often a change of self is needed more than a change of scene.

Efficiency is increased not by what we accomplish, but more by what we relinquish.

The closest to perfection that we ever come is when we fill out a job application.

When we are out of touch with ourselves, we cannot touch others.

Go ahead with your life, your plans. Don't waste time by stopping before the interruptions have started.

RICHARD EVANS

A foolish act done over again will not improve things.

WEST AFRICAN PROVERB

In a Perfect World

A person would feel as good at 50 as she did at 17, and she would actually be as smart at 50 as she thought she was at 17.

You could give away a baby bed without getting pregnant.

Doing what was good for you would be what you enjoyed doing the most.

People would always have reasons to be optimistic.

The mail would always be early, the check would always be in the mail, and it would be written for more than you expected.

Potato chips might have calories, but if you ate them with dip, the calories would be neutralized.

Winning might be a nice thing, but that would be all.

The better the food tasted, the fewer calories it would have.

Warranties would be for 13 months and products would fail at 12 months.

"Two Friends"
Lanie, 11 years old.

For Those Who Take Life Too Seriously

1. On the other hand, you have different fingers.
2. Forty-two percent of all statistics are made up on the spot.
3. I feel like I'm diagonally parked in a parallel universe.
4. The early bird may get the worm, but the second mouse gets the cheese.
5. I drive way too fast to worry about cholesterol.
6. Bills travel through the mail at twice the speed of checks.
7. The sooner you fall behind, the more time you'll have to catch up.
8. Change is inevitable except from vending machines.
9. If at first you don't succeed, then skydiving isn't for you.

Author unknown

Warning: Laughter may be hazardous to your illness.

NURSES FOR LAUGHTER

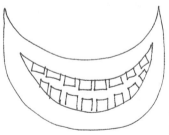

"Smile"
Carrie, 25 years old.

The secret to life is sneakers—you have to keep moving to stay comfortable.

CARL HAMMERSCHAG, M.D.

Never let the fear of striking out get in your way.

BABE RUTH

Heard on a public transportation vehicle in Orlando:
"When you exit this vehicle, please be sure to lower your head and watch your step. If you fail to do so, please lower your voice and watch your language. Thank you."

If you eat your bagel, you'll have nothing in your pocket but the hole.

YIDDISH PROVERB

Do not wait for leaders; do it alone, person to person.

MOTHER TERESA

As you make your way through this hectic world of ours, set aside a few minutes each day. At the end of the year, you'll have a couple of days saved up.

ANONYMOUS

Cocoon

A man found a caterpillar's cocoon. One day a small opening appeared. The man sat and watched the butterfly for several hours as it struggled to force its body through the little hole. It seemed to stop

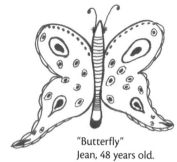

"Butterfly"
Jean, 48 years old.

making any progress. It appeared to have gotten as far as it could. It apparently could go no further.

The man decided to help the butterfly. He took a pair of scissors and snipped off the remaining bit of the cocoon.

The butterfly emerged easily, but it had a swollen body and small, shriveled wings. The man continued to watch the butterfly. He expected that, at any moment, the wings would enlarge and support the butterfly's body. It never happened! In fact, the butterfly spent the rest of its life crawling around with a swollen body and shriveled wings. It could not fly.

The man, in his kindness and haste, did not understand that nature made the restricting cocoon. The struggle required for the butterfly to get through the tiny opening forces fluid from the butterfly's body into its wings. It becomes ready to fly as it emerges from the cocoon.

We are like the caterpillar in the cocoon. Although we often cannot make sense of it, struggles can be exactly what we need in our life. If we go through our life without any obstacles, we do not fully develop. If some well-intentioned person breaks the cocoon open too soon, we will not flourish. As difficult as it is to watch someone you care for struggle, our true friends respect our pain and comfort us. But they do not do our work for us. Because if they did, we would not be as strong as we can be.

And we could never learn to fly.

Author unknown

> *Be bold. If you're going to make an error, make a doozy, and don't be afraid to hit the ball.*
>
> BILLIE JEAN KING

The Present

Imagine there is a bank that credits your account each morning with $86,400.

It carries over no balance from day to day. Every evening the bank deletes whatever part of the balance you failed to use during the day.

What would you do? Draw out every cent of course!!!

Each of us has such a bank; its name is TIME. Every morning, it credits you with 86,400 seconds. Every night it writes off, as lost, whatever you failed to invest to good purpose.

It carries over no balance. It allows no overdraft. Each day it opens a new account for you. Each night it burns the remains of the day. If you fail to use the day's deposits, the loss is yours.

There is no going back. There is no drawing against the "tomorrow." You must live in the present on today's deposits. Invest it so as to get from it the utmost in health, happiness, and success! The clock is running. Make the most of today.

Anonymous

> *To get them to listen, get them laughing.*
>
> ALLEN KLEIN
>
> *Have fun...misery is optional.*
>
> ANONYMOUS

Instructions for Life

1. Give people more than they expect and do it cheerfully.
2. Memorize your favorite poem.
3. When you say, "I love you," mean it.
4. When you say, "I'm sorry," look the person in the eye.
5. Never laugh at anyone's dreams.
6. Love deeply and passionately. You might get hurt, but it's the only way to live life completely.
7. Talk slowly but think quickly.
8. When someone asks you a question you don't want to answer, smile and ask, "Why do you want to know?"
9. Remember that great love and great achievements involve great risk.
10. Call your mom.
11. Say "Excuse me" when you bump into someone.
12. When you lose, don't lose the lesson.
13. Remember the three R's: Respect for self; Respect for others; Responsibility for all your actions.
14. Don't let a little dispute injure a great friendship.
15. When you realize you've made a mistake, take immediate steps to correct it.
16. Smile when picking up the phone. The caller will hear it in your voice.

17. Marry a man or woman whom you love to talk to. As you get older, their conversational skills will be as important as any others.
18. Spend some time alone.
19. Open your arms to change, but don't let go of your values.
20. Remember that silence is sometimes the best answer.
21. Read more books and watch less TV.
22. Live a good, honorable life. Then when you get older and think back, you can enjoy it a second time.
23. A loving atmosphere in your home is so important. Do all you can to create a tranquil, harmonious home.
24. In disagreements with loved ones, deal with the current situation. Don't bring up the past.
25. Read between the lines.
26. Humbly share your knowledge. It's a way to achieve immortality.
27. Be gentle with the earth.
28. Never interrupt when you are being flattered.
29. Once a year, go someplace you've never been before.
30. If you make a lot of money, put it to use helping others while you are living. That is wealth's greatest satisfaction.
31. Remember that not getting what you want is sometimes a stroke of luck.
32. Learn the rules, then break some.
33. Remember that the best relationship is one where your love for each other is greater than your need for each other.
34. Remember that your character is your destiny.
35. Approach love and cooking with reckless abandon.

Anonymous

The Importance of Time

To realize the value of ONE YEAR, ask a student who failed a grade.

To realize the value of ONE MONTH, ask a mother who gave birth to a premature baby.

To realize the value of ONE WEEK, ask the editor of a weekly newspaper.

To realize the value of ONE HOUR, ask lovers who are waiting to meet.

To realize the value of ONE MINUTE, ask a person who missed the train.

To realize the value of ONE SECOND, ask a person who just avoided an accident.

To realize the value of ONE MILLISECOND, ask the person who won a silver medal in the Olympics.

Treasure every moment that you have!

And remember that time waits for no one.

Yesterday is history. Tomorrow is a mystery.

Today is a gift. That is why it is called the present.

Anonymous

The idea of strictly minding our own business is moldy rubbish. Who could be so selfish?

MYRTIE BARKER

You really can change the world if you care enough.

MARIAN WRIGHT EDELMAN

Practice Your ABC's

Act silly
Believe in magic
Create your own masterpieces
Daydream every chance you get
Explore a book
Find time for fun
Give hugs
Hang upside down from trees
Imagine
Join clubs
Keep it simple
Love all creatures
Make time for friends
Nap when you can
Open your mind to new ideas
Play when you feel like it
Question the answers
Run with the wind
Sing favorite songs
Take days off
Uncover your talents
Venture out
Walk on the wild side
X-pect the best
Yield to the moment
Zzzz peacefully at night

Anonymous

"Clock"; Sofia, 10 years old.

Your own stories

"Girl"
Kaitlyn, 6 years old.

Aging

Two thoughts come to mind when I think about the aging process: it is inevitable and it will come sooner than you want it to. We hear all of the clichés about growing older, such as "growing older gracefully" and "aging like a fine wine." One thing that is necessary to make this life passage a little more tolerable is a sense of humor. We have to be able to laugh at ourselves and with each other.

One of my favorite quotes about the aging process is, "Inside every older person is a young person saying 'What the hell happened to me?'"

I remember when I was a child and my mother was 35 years old. I thought she was soooo old. Then I reached, and flew by, 35. Now it seems sooooo young.

When we age, we have a right of passage that allows us to do things that younger people can't do. We can be more honest. We can forget things more often. My favorite privilege is the right to take more naps.

Act silly! People will simply excuse your behavior because you are older now. But have fun with life. You don't have to become more serious as you grow older; your prescription could simply read: Joke, laugh, and have fun living each day to its fullest.

✳ ✳ ✳

How to Know You're Getting Older
Everything hurts.

And what doesn't hurt, doesn't work.

You feel like the morning after, and you haven't been anywhere.

You join the health club and don't go.

You need your glasses to find your glasses.

Your back goes out more than you do.

Your knees buckle but your belt won't.

Your mind makes contracts your body can't meet.

Dialing long distance wears you out.

Your children begin to look middle aged.

The gleam in your eyes is from the sun hitting your bifocals.

You look forward to a dull evening.

You know all the answers, but nobody asks you the questions.

You have too much room in the house but not enough in the medicine chest.

You stop looking forward to your next birthday, but you're glad when it arrives!

> *Life is a marvelous, transitory adventure.*
>
> NIKKI GIOVANNI

"Blanket"
Lanie, 11 years old.

To Whom It May Concern

I am officially tendering my resignation as an adult, in order to accept the responsibilities of a 6-year-old. The tax base is lower.

I want to be six again.

I want to sail sticks across a fresh mud puddle and make waves with rocks.

I want to think M&Ms are better than money, because you can eat them.

I want to play kickball during recess and stay up on Christmas Eve, waiting to hear Santa and Rudolph on the roof.

I long for the days when life was simple. When all I knew

were my colors, the addition tables, and simple nursery rhymes, but it didn't bother me, because I didn't know what I didn't know and I didn't care.

I want to go to school and have snack time, recess, gym, and field trips.

I want to think the world is fair and everyone in it is honest and good.

I want to believe that anything is possible.

Sometimes, while I was maturing, I learned too much. I learned of nuclear weapons, prejudice, starving and abused kids, lies, unhappy marriages, illness, pain, and mortality.

I want to be six again.

I want to think that everyone, including myself, will live forever because I don't know the concept of death. I want to be oblivious to the complexity of life and be overly excited by the little things again.

I want television to be something I watch for fun, not something I use for escape from the things I should be doing.

I want to live knowing the little things that I find exciting will always make me as happy as when I first learned them.

I want to be six again.

I want to walk down the beach and think only of the sand beneath my feet and the possibility of finding that blue piece of sea glass I'm looking for.

"Hi"; Lairen, 9 years old.

I want to spend my afternoons climbing trees and riding my bike, letting the grownups worry about time, the dentist, and how to find the money to fix the old car.

I want to wonder what I'll do when I grow up, and what I'll be, and who I'll be, and not worry about what I'll do if this doesn't work out.

I want that time back.

I want to use it now as an escape, so that when my computer crashes, or I have a mountain of paperwork, or two depressed friends, or a fight with my spouse, or bittersweet memories of times gone by, or second thoughts about so many things, I can travel back and build a snowman, without thinking about anything except whether the snow sticks together and what I can possibly use for the snowman's mouth.

I want to be six again.

Author unknown

You don't stop laughing because you grow old, you grow old because you stop laughing.

MICHAEL PRITCHARD

You Know You're Getting Older When...
Your potted plants stay alive.
You keep more food than beer in the fridge.
You have to pay your own credit card bill.
Mac and cheese no longer counts as a well-balanced meal.
You haven't seen a soap opera in over a year.
8 a.m. is not early.

You have to file your own taxes.

You hear your favorite song on the elevator at work.

You're not carded anymore.

You carry an umbrella.

Your friends marry and divorce instead of hook up and break up.

You start watching the weather channel.

You go from 130 days of vacation time to seven.

You stop confusing "401(k) plan" with "10K run."

Your parents and other adults feel comfortable telling jokes about sex in front of you.

You don't know what time Burger King closes anymore.

You don't care where your spouse goes—as long as you don't have to go along.

Your car insurance premium goes down.

You refer to college students as kids.

Your parents start making casual remarks about grandchildren.

You feed your dog Science Diet instead of Taco Bell.

You're sitting in a rocker and you can't get it started.

You wake up with that morning-after feeling, and you didn't do anything the night before.

You stop buying green bananas.

Minds are like parachutes: They only function when open.

THOMAS DEWAR

Things to Look Forward to as You Get Older
  You get asked for ID to prove that you are old enough to
    qualify for a senior discount.
  Once you retire you can never get fired.
  A pint of ice cream lasts a month.
  No more scares about pregnancy.
  Your children start to like you again.
  You don't have to stand when someone stops by the table to
    greet you.
  You can wear a funny hat, thongs, and a bathrobe to the
    beach.
  You have earned the right to order rice pudding when eating
    at the cafeteria.
  Having grandchildren helps make not having grandparents
    easier.
  If you are on a sinking ship, you will be saved with the
    women and children.
  People get out of your way when you drive down the street.
  People pick up the things you drop.
  Men can save money on shampoo.

✳ ✳ ✳

There are three signs of old age. The first is your loss of
memory, and the other two I forget.

Middle age is when work is a lot less fun—and fun is a lot
more work.

Statistics show that at the age of 70, there are five women to every man. Isn't that the darndest time for a guy to get those odds?

Middle age is when it takes longer to rest than to get tired.

By the time people are wise enough to watch their step, they are too old to go anywhere.

A man has reached middle age when he is cautioned to slow down by his doctor instead of by the police.

You know you're into middle age when you realize that caution is the only thing you care to exercise.

Pearly Gates

A couple, both 85 years old, died in a car crash. They had been married for almost 60 years. They had been in good health for the last 15 years, mainly because the old woman took an interest in health foods and exercise.

When they reached the pearly gates, St. Peter took them to their mansion. It included a beautiful kitchen, a wrap-around deck, a movie-screen-sized TV, and a master bedroom suite with a whirlpool.

As they looked around, the old man asked St. Peter, "How much is all of this going to cost?"

"Nothing," replied St. Peter. "This is heaven."

Next they went out to the back yard to survey the champion-style golf course that adjoined their property. They had all club privileges. Once a week the course changed to duplicate one of the world's greatest courses.

The old man asked, "What are the greens fees?"

St. Peter said, "This is heaven. You play for free."

Next they went to the club house. There they saw a lavish buffet with foods from all over the world.

"How much to eat?" asked the old man.

"Don't you understand yet? This is heaven. It is free!" replied St. Peter, somewhat frustrated.

"Well, where are the low-fat and low-cholesterol tables?" the old man asked timidly.

St. Peter responded, "That's the best part. You can eat as much as you like—of whatever you like—and never get fat or sick. This is heaven!"

When he heard that news, the old man became very angry. He

"Angel"
Leah, 9 years old.

threw down his hat and stomped on it, screaming wildly. St. Peter and his wife both tried to calm him down. "What's wrong?" they asked.

The old man looked at his wife and said, "This is all your fault. If it weren't for your blasted bran muffins and tofu, I could have been here 15 years ago!"

Author unknown

The cardiologist's diet: If it tastes good, spit it out.

Doctor to patient: "I have good news and bad news. The good news is that you are not a hypochondriac."

Wisdom from Senior Citizens
1. I finally got my head together and now my body is falling apart.
2. It is easier to get older than it is to get wiser.
3. Funny, I don't remember being absent minded.
4. If God had wanted me to touch my toes, She would have put them on my knees.
5. If you are living on the edge, make sure you are wearing your seat belt.
6. It's not the pace of life that concerns me, it's the sudden stop at the end.
7. If all is not lost, where is it?
8. When did my wild oats turn into prunes and bran muffins?
9. If at first you don't succeed, redefine success.

Reverse Living
Life is tough.
It takes up a lot of your time,
all of your weekends,
and what do you get at the end of it?
.....Death, a great reward.

I think that the life cycle is all backwards.
You should die first, get it out of the way.
Then you live 20 years in an old age home.
You get kicked out when you're too young,
you get a gold watch and you go to work.
You work 40 years until you're
young enough to enjoy your retirement.
You go to college,
you party until you're ready for high school,
you become a little kid, you play,
you have no responsibilities,
you become a little girl or boy,
you go back into the womb,
and you spend your last nine months floating.
And you finish off as a gleam in someone's eye.

Author unknown

God grant me the senility
To forget the people who
I never liked anyway.
The good fortune to run into the ones I do.
And the eyesight to tell the difference.

What I've Learned

I like my teacher because she cries when we sing "Silent Night." *Age 6*

You can't hide a piece of broccoli in a glass of milk. *Age 7*

When I wave to people in the country, they stop what they are doing and wave back. *Age 9*

Just when I get my room the way I like it, Mom makes me clean it up. *Age 13*

If you want to cheer yourself up, you should try cheering someone else up. *Age 14*

Although it's hard to admit it, I'm secretly glad my parents are strict with me. *Age 15*

Silent company is often more healing than words of advice. *Age 24*

"Mommy"
Devin,
9½ years old.

Brushing my child's hair is one of life's great pleasures. *Age 26*

Wherever I go, the world's worst drivers follow me there. *Age 29*

If someone says something unkind about me, I must live so that no one will believe it. *Age 39*

There are people who love you dearly but just don't know how to show it. *Age 41*

You can make someone's day by simply sending a little card. *Age 44*

The greater a person's sense of guilt, the greater his need to cast blame on others. *Age 46*

Children and grandparents are natural allies. *Age 47*

Singing "Amazing Grace" can lift my spirits for hours. *Age 49*

Motel mattresses are better on the side away from the phone. *Age 50*

You can tell a lot about a man by the way he handles these three things: a rainy day, lost luggage, and tangled Christmas tree lights. *Age 52*

Keeping a vegetable garden is worth a medicine cabinet full of pills. *Age 52*

Regardless of your relationship with your parents, you miss them terribly after they die. *Age 53*

Making a living is not the same thing as making a life. *Age 58*

If you want to do something positive for your children, try to improve your marriage. *Age 61*

Life sometimes gives you a second chance. *Age 62*

You shouldn't go through life with catchers' mitts on both hands. You need to be able to throw something back. *Age 64*

If you pursue happiness, it will elude you. But if you focus on your family, the needs of others, your work, meeting new people, and doing the very best you can, happiness will find you. *Age 65*

Whenever I decide something with kindness, I usually make the right decision. *Age 66*

Everyone can use a prayer. *Age 72*

It pays to believe in miracles. And to tell the truth, I've seen several. *Age 73*

Even when I have pains, I don't have to be one. *Age 82*

Every day you should reach out and touch someone. People love that human touch—holding hands, a warm hug, or just a friendly pat on the back. *Age 85*

I've learned that I still have a lot to learn. *Age 92*

Author unknown

I was speaking with some residents of an assisted living complex in our town. I asked them what advice they might have for me to pass on to younger people. Helen said, quite seriously and then with a big smile, "Tell them to have younger friends when they get old, or everyone will be dead and they won't have anyone to talk to."

Life is like riding a bicycle. You don't fall off unless you stop pedaling.

Do you know the definition of middle age? It's when you choose your cereal for the fiber and not for the toy.

Signs That You Are No Longer a Kid

You're asleep, but others worry that you're dead.

You can live without sex, but not without glasses.

You buy a compass for the dash of your car.

You quit trying to hold your stomach in, no matter who walks into the room.

You are proud of your lawn mower.

Your best friend is dating someone half their age and isn't breaking any laws.

Your arms are almost too short to read the newspaper.

You sing along with the elevator music.

You constantly talk about the price of gasoline.

You enjoy hearing about other people's operations.

You no longer think of speed limits as a challenge.

People call at 9 p.m. and ask, "Did I wake you?"

You have a dream about prunes.

You answer a question with "Because I said so!"

You send money to PBS.

The end of your tie doesn't come anywhere near the top of your pants.

You take a metal detector to the beach.

You can't remember the last time you lay on the floor to watch television.

You get into a heated argument about pension plans.

You got cable for the weather channel.

You have a party and the neighbors don't even realize it.

Your own stories

_____

_____

_____

_____

_____

_____

_____

_____

_____

_____

_____

_____

_____

_____

_____

_____

_____

_____

_____

_____

_____

_____

"A Dog"
Alyson, 5 years old.

Dogs

When I began sharing funny cartoons at my stress reduction presentations, I used an overhead called, "The 17 Ways to Be a Happy Dog." I was amazed how many people asked for copies of that overhead. I learned that I am not the only person who loves dogs.

When I left my last job, I considered opening "Yuppie Puppy Dog Care Center." The main reason that I didn't was that I knew I wouldn't have the heart to tell the "parents" if their dog had a bad day.

When I drive around my hometown with my cocker, a friend's dog, and my daughter's dog, people smile and tell me what a nice family I have. The people at the bank have treats ready. The dogs begin to drool all over the window at their first glimpse of the bank sign. The whole town loves dogs!

I will never forget when my dog Shasta was sick. The vet told me to make her a mixture of rice and hamburger. My young children said, "Can we have this hot dish you made?"

"No!" I responded. "That is for the dog. We're having tomato soup." I am sure they often thought the dog got better treatment than they did.

Some people call my friend Vicki and me eccentric. I think that's because on Memorial Day weekend we have a birthday party for our cockers. We have treats, hats, games, and a special cake. I know that we are not the only people absurd enough to go to these measures to care for our dogs, but it does cause some folks to question our sanity. As you can see, dogs are an important part of my life.

They are assets to many other people also. We get close to them, bond with them, and then have to let them go. Dogs live in many adult care centers because they give people a connection to something outside of themselves. Petting dogs lowers blood pressure. Dogs bring children of all ages comfort and friendship. Dogs definitely help us to lighten up and live longer.

This chapter is a tribute to our four-legged, barking, loving, slobbering, loyal friends.

※　※　※

If...
If you can start your day without caffeine,

If you can always be cheerful, ignoring aches and pains,

If you can resist complaining and boring people with your troubles,

"Dog"; Vicki, 47 years old.

If you can overlook it when those you love take it out on you when, through no fault of yours, something goes wrong,

If you can ignore a friend's limited education and never correct them,

If you can resist treating a rich friend better than a poor friend,

If you can face the world without lies and deceit,

If you can conquer tension without medical help,

If you can relax without booze,

If you can say honestly that deep in your heart you have no prejudice against creed, color, religion, or politics —

THEN you are as good as your dog.

Anonymous

Two dogs are standing on their back legs looking at a small box sitting next to the telephone.

One dog says to the other dog, "They call this thing 'Caller ID.' It's sort of an electronic butt sniffing device."

Fourteen Simple Rules for Being a Happy Dog

1. If it moves — chase it.
2. If it doesn't move — chew on it.
3. If it makes noise — bark at it.
4. If it is bigger than you — jump on it.
5. If they say "Get Down!" — jump on it.
6. If it is clean — soil it.
7. If it is dirty — hide it.
8. If they catch you — look ashamed.
9. If they are angry — look incurably cute.

10. If they tell you to eat it — refuse.
11. If they tell you not to eat it — eat it when they aren't looking.
12. If they tell you it's bedtime — it's time to play.
13. Hang out with children — they operate by the same rules.
14. Above all else, remember you are the one in charge — never let them forget who is the boss.

> *I myself have known some profoundly thoughtful dogs.*
>
> JAMES THURBER

Dugan, my daughter's black lab, eats twice a day—early in the morning and again in the evening.

One day around 11 a.m., Nick, who is 3½, began to give Dugan a new bowl of dog food.

His dad said, "Nick, don't feed Dugan now. He already had breakfast."

Nick retorted, "But he must be hungry. He just tried to eat my cookie."

> *Dogs' lives are too short. Their only fault, really.*
>
> ELIZABETH BOWEN

Things Dogs Have to Remember

I will not play tug-of-war with Dad's underwear when he is on the toilet.

The garbage collector is NOT stealing our stuff.

I must shake the rainwater out of my fur BEFORE entering the house.

The diaper pail is not a cookie jar.

I will not chew on crayons or pens, especially not the red ones, or my people will think I am bleeding.

The sofa is not a face towel. Neither are Mom and Dad's laps.

My head does not belong in the refrigerator.

We do not have a doorbell; I will not bark each time I hear one on TV.

I will not eat the cat's food, either before OR after he eats it.

I will not roll on dead seagulls, fish, or crabs.

Doggy Wisdom

Why eat dog food when people food is available?

A great way to get more people food is to make friends with the kids.

Be sure to do the cat-chasing after Mom and Dad have left the house.

"Dog"
Mackie, 6 years old.

Shake and whimper at the vet and your people will pet you the entire time you're there.

People beds are much more comfortable than doggy beds.

There is always plenty of cold water in the toilet bowl.

Sweep everything off low-lying tables at least once a day.

If you're big, learn to slobber. If you're small, learn to yip.

Squirrels are for barking. Cats are for chasing. People are for licking.

Kids need to know how to do tricks. Teach them how to throw a ball.

Bark at falling leaves. Bark at birds. Bark at all possible occasions. Everyone loves the sound of your voice.

Practice making noise with your squeaky toy in the middle of the night. People notice and it's much more fun.

"No" means "Maybe," unless it is shouted.

Lick the kids' faces. There might be food on them.

A cold nose is a great introduction.

The can opener is your friend. Come running every time you hear it.

Keep your tail tucked under your belly so the little people won't grab it.

Never let them take your ball without a good game of tug.

"Dog"
Libby, 9 years old.

Toddlers put everything in their mouths, so watch your tail!

Never admit that you're too old to be a puppy.

No matter what your age, size, or breed, you're never too big to be a lap dog.

Life Lessons from Dogs

Don't go out without an "ID."

Be direct with people; let them know exactly how you feel by piddling on their shoes.

Be aware of when to hold your tongue and when to use it.

Leave room in your schedule for a good nap.

When you do something wrong, always take responsibility (as soon as you're dragged out from under the bed).

If it's not wet and sloppy, it's not a real kiss.

Dogs are the most amazing creatures; they give unconditional love. For me they are the role model for being alive.

GILDA RADNER

Buy a pup and your money will buy love unflinching.

RICHARD KIPLING

Dog Rules

1. The dog is not allowed in the house.
2. Okay, the dog is allowed in the house, but only in

certain rooms.

3. The dog is allowed in all rooms, but has to stay off the furniture.
4. The dog can get on the old furniture only.
5. Fine, the dog is allowed on all the furniture, but is not allowed to sleep with the humans on the bed.
6. Okay, the dog is allowed on the bed, but only by invitation.
7. The dog can sleep on the bed whenever he wants, but not under the covers.
8. The dog can sleep under the covers by invitation only.
9. The dog can sleep under the covers every night.
10. Humans must ask permission to sleep under the covers with the dog.

Famous Quotes about Dogs

Our dogs will love and admire the meanest of us, and feed our colossal vanity with their uncritical homage.

AGNES REPPLIER

Scratch a dog and you'll find a permanent job.

FRANKLIN P. JONES

There is no dog so bad but he will wag his tail.

ITALIAN PROVERB

Puppies are nature's remedy for feeling unloved...plus a remedy for numerous other ailments of life.

RICHARD ALLAN PALM

The misery of keeping a dog is his dying so soon. But, to be sure, if he lived for 50 years and then died, what would become of me?

SIR WALTER SCOTT

A dog teaches a boy fidelity, perseverance, and to turn around three times before lying down.

ROBERT BENCHLEY

There is no such thing as a difficult dog, only an inexperienced owner.

BARBARA WOODHOUSE

Dogs act exactly the way that we would act if we had no shame.

CYNTHIA HEIMEL

Children and dogs are as necessary to the welfare of the country as Wall Street and the railroads.

HARRY S. TRUMAN

Dog lovers are a good breed themselves.

GLADYS TABER

I love a dog. He does nothing for political reasons.

WILL ROGERS

Help Wanted

A local business, looking for office help, put a "Help Wanted" sign in the window. "Must be able to type, must be good with a computer, and must be bilingual. We are an Equal Opportunity Employer."

A short time afterwards, a dog trotted up to the window, saw the sign, and went inside. He looked at the receptionist and wagged his tail, then walked over to the sign, looked at it, and whined.

Getting the idea, the receptionist got the office manager. The office manager looked at the dog and was surprised, to say the least.

However, the dog looked determined, so he led him into the office.

Inside, the dog jumped up on the chair and stared at the manager. The manager said, "I can't hire you. The sign says you have to be able to type."

The dog jumped down, went to the typewriter, and proceeded to type out a perfect letter. He took out the page, trotted over to the manager, and gave it to him, then jumped back on the chair. The manager was stunned, but then told the dog, "The sign says you have to be good with a computer."

The dog jumped down again and went to the computer. He proceeded to enter and execute a perfect program that worked flawlessly the first time.

By this time the manager was totally dumbfounded! He looked at the dog and said, "I realize that you are a very intelligent dog and have some interesting abilities. However, I still can't give you the job." The dog jumped down and went to a copy of the sign and put his paw on the sentence that told about being an Equal Opportunity Employer.

The manager said, "Yes, but the sign also says that you have to be bilingual."

The dog looked at the manager calmly and said, "Meow."

"Dog"
Alisha, 9 years old.

Mind Games that Dogs Play with Humans

1. After your humans give you a bath, DON'T LET THEM TOWEL DRY YOU! Instead, run to their bed, jump up, and dry yourself off on the sheets. This game is especially good if it's right before your humans' bedtime.

2. When the humans come home, put your ears back, tail between your legs, and chin down. Act as if you have done something really bad. Then, watch as the humans frantically

search the house for the damage they think you have caused. (Note: This game only works when you have done absolutely nothing wrong.)

3. Let the humans teach you a brand new trick. Learn it perfectly. Then, when the humans want you to demonstrate it to someone else, stare blankly. Pretend you have no idea what they're talking about.

4. Make your humans be patient. When you go outside to pee, sniff around the entire yard as your humans wait. Act as if the spot you choose to go pee will ultimately decide the fate of the earth.

5. Draw attention to the human. When out for a walk always pick the busiest, most visible spot to go pee. Take your time and make sure everyone watches. This game works particularly well if your humans have forgotten to bring a plastic bag.

6. When out for a walk, alternate between choking and coughing every time a strange human walks by.

7. Make your own rules. Don't always bring back the stick when playing fetch with humans. Make them go and chase it once in a while.

8. Hide from your humans. When your humans come home, don't greet them at the door. Instead, hide from them, and make them think something terrible has happened to you. Don't reappear until one of your humans is panic-stricken and close to tears.

9. When your human calls you to come back in, always take your time. Walk as slowly as possible back to the door.

10. Wake up twenty minutes before the alarm clock is set to go off. Make the humans take you out for your morning pee. As

soon as you get back inside, fall asleep. Humans can rarely fall back asleep after going outside. This game will drive them nuts!

Things We Can Learn from a Dog

1. Never pass up an opportunity to go for a joyride.
2. Allow the experience of fresh air and the wind in your face to be pure ecstasy.
3. When a loved one comes home, always run to greet them.
4. When it's in your best interest, practice obedience.
5. Let others know when they've invaded your territory.
6. Take naps and stretch before rising.
7. Run, romp, and play daily.
8. Eat with gusto and enthusiasm.
9. Be loyal.
10. Never pretend to be something you're not.
11. If what you want lies buried, dig until you find it.
12. When someone is having a bad day, be silent, sit close by, and nuzzle them gently.
13. Thrive on attention and let people touch you.
14. Avoid biting when a simple growl will do.
15. On hot days, drink lots of water and lie under a shady tree.
16. When you're happy, dance around and wag your entire body.
17. No matter how often you're scolded, don't buy into the guilt thing and pout...run right back and make new friends.
18. Delight in the simple joy of a long walk.

Your own stories

_____

_____

_____

_____

_____

_____

_____

_____

_____

_____

_____

_____

_____

_____

_____

_____

_____

_____

_____

_____

_____

"Grandma"; Olivia, 4 years old.

Wisdom

As you browsed through the Table of Contents of this book, you may have wondered what wisdom has to do with humor. In this chapter you will find stories and articles passed on to me by friends and colleagues. Each written piece gave me something new to think about, and learn from, to develop wisdom from the light side.

Wisdom doesn't always have to be intellectual. It often also involves our emotions. Tears and laughter can take us to our own inner wisdom. You can pass on to others the thought-provoking, sometimes emotionally touching stories and anecdotes in this chapter. Some anecdotes you may have seen before, while others will be new to you. Whatever the case, I hope you enjoy the following stories and fill the blank pages at the end of this chapter with wisdom that others have passed on to you.

(S)He who laughs—lasts!

ANONYMOUS

The art of medicine consists of amusing the patient while nature cures the disease.

VOLTAIRE

People

People important to you and people unimportant to you cross your life, touch it with love or carelessness, and move on.

There are people who leave you, and you breathe a sigh of relief and wonder why you ever came in contact with them.

There are people who leave you, and you breathe a sigh of memories and wonder why they had to go away and leave such a gaping hole.

Children leave parents, friends leave friends, acquaintances move on. People change homes. People grow apart. Enemies hate and move on. Friends love and move on.

You look at those present and wonder. I believe in God's master plan in life. He moves people in and out of each other's lives, and each leaves his mark on the other.

You find you are made up of bits and pieces of all who ever touched your life, and you are more because of it and you would be less if they had not touched you.

Thank you for touching my life.

When humor goes—there goes civilization.

ERMA BOMBECK

> *Blessed are they who laugh at themselves.*
> *They will never cease to be entertained.*

CHINESE PROVERB

Smile

She smiled at the sorrowful stranger.
The smile seemed to make him feel better.
He remembered past kindnesses of a friend
And wrote him a thank-you letter.
The friend was so pleased with the thank-you
That he left a large tip after lunch.
The server, surprised by the size of the tip,
Bet the whole thing on a hunch.
The next day she picked up her winnings,
And gave part to a man on the street.
The man on the street was grateful;
For two days he'd had nothing to eat.
After he finished his dinner,
He left for his small, dingy room.
He didn't know at that moment that he might be facing
his doom.
On the way he picked up a shivering puppy
And took him home to get warm.
The puppy was very grateful
To be in out of the storm.
That night the house caught on fire.
The puppy barked the alarm.
He barked till he woke the whole household
And saved everybody from harm.

One of the boys that he rescued
Grew up to be President.
All this because of a simple smile
That hadn't cost a cent.

Anonymous

"Teeth (in a mouth)"
Devin, 9½ years old.

Success

To laugh often and much.

To win the respect of intelligent people and the affection of children.

To earn the appreciation of honest critics and endure the betrayal of false friends.

To appreciate beauty and to find the best in others.

To leave the world a bit better, whether by a healthy child, a garden patch, or a redeemed social condition.

To know even one life has breathed easier because you have lived.

This is to have succeeded.

Ralph Waldo Emerson

> *People who don't laugh at work fall into tunnel vision. They are not as open to creative solutions.*
>
> JOEL GOODMAN

The Meaning of Peace

There once was a king who offered a prize to the artist who could paint the best picture of peace. Many artists tried. The king looked at all the pictures. There were two he really liked and he had to choose between them.

One picture was of a calm lake. The lake was a perfect mirror for the peaceful, towering mountains that were all around it. Overhead was a blue sky with fluffy white clouds. All who saw this picture thought that it was the perfect picture of peace.

The other picture had mountains too. But these mountains were rugged and bare. Above them was an angry sky from which rain fell, and lightning flashed. Down the side of the mountain tumbled a wild, foaming waterfall. This picture did not look peaceful at all, everyone said.

But when the king looked closely, he saw behind the water-fall a tiny bush growing in a crack in the rock. In the bush a mother bird had built her nest. There, in the midst of the rush of angry water, sat the mother bird on her nest.

Which picture do you think won the prize for perfect peace?

The king named the second picture the winner. Do you know why?

"Because," explained the king, "peace does not mean to be in a place where there is no noise, trouble, or hard work. Peace means to be in the midst of all those things and still be calm in your heart. That is the real meaning of peace."

Author unknown

The Independent Princess

Once upon a time, in a land far away, a beautiful, independent, self-assured princess met up with a frog. She sat contemplating ecological issues on the shores of an unpolluted pond in a verdant meadow near her castle.

The frog hopped into the princess's lap and said, "Elegant Lady, I was once a handsome prince, until an evil witch cast a spell upon me. One kiss from you, however, and I will turn back into the dapper young prince that I was. And then, my sweet, we can marry and set up housekeeping in your castle. My mother can live with us. You can prepare my meals, clean my clothes, bear my children, and forever feel grateful and happy doing so."

The princess chuckled to herself as she thought, "I don't think so."

That night, she dined sumptuously on a repast of lightly sautéed frog legs seasoned in a white wine cream sauce.

Author unknown

Keep Your Fork

There once was a woman whom the doctors diagnosed with a terminal illness. They gave her three months to live. After hearing the news, she began to plan her funeral. She contacted her pastor. He came to her house to discuss her final wishes.

She told him which songs she would like to have at the service, what scriptures she would like read, and what outfit she wanted to be buried in. The woman also requested to be buried with her favorite Bible. Thinking that all of the details were covered, the pastor prepared to leave. The woman suddenly remembered something very important to her.

"There's one more thing," she said excitedly.

"What's that?" asked the pastor.

"This is very important," the woman continued. "I want to be buried with a fork in my right hand."

"Fork"
Grazelle,
79 years old.

The pastor looked at the woman, not knowing quite what to say.

"That surprises you, doesn't it?" the woman asked.

"Well, to be honest, I'm puzzled by the request," said the pastor.

The woman explained, "In all my years of attending church dinners, whoever cleared the main dishes would inevitably lean over and say, 'Keep your fork.' It was my favorite part of the dinner because I knew that something better was coming—like velvety chocolate cake or deep-dish apple pie. Something wonderful, and with substance! So, I just want people to see me there in that casket with a fork in my hand. I want them to wonder 'What's with the fork?' Then I want you to tell them, 'Keep your fork. The best is yet to come.'"

The pastor's eyes welled up as he hugged the woman good-bye. He knew this would be one of the last times he would see her alive. He also knew that the woman had a better grasp of heaven than he did. She knew that something better was coming.

As the pastor and those who attended the wise woman's wake will never forget her lesson, may you learn from her also. The next time you reach down for your fork, let it remind you that the best is yet to come.

Author unknown

Hugs

There's something in a simple hug that always warms the heart.
It welcomes us back home and makes it easier to part.
A hug's a way to share the joy and sad times we go through,
Or just a way for friends to say they like you—'cause you're you.
Hugs are meant for anyone for whom we really care,
From your grandma to your neighbor, or a cuddly teddy bear.
A hug is an amazing thing—it's just the perfect way
To show the love we're feeling but can't find the words to say.
It's funny how a little hug makes everyone feel good;
In every place and language, it's always understood.
And hugs don't need new equipment, special batteries or parts;
Just open up your arms and open up your hearts.

Anonymous

An Angel Wrote

Many people will walk in and out of your life,
but only true friends will leave footprints in your heart.
To handle yourself, use your head;
To handle others, use your heart.
Anger is only one letter short of danger.
God gives every bird its food,
But He does not throw it into its nest.
He who loses money, loses much;
He who loses a friend, loses more;
He who loses faith, loses all.
Beautiful young people are acts of nature,
But beautiful old people are works of art.

Learn from the mistakes of others.
You can't live long enough to make
them all yourself.
Friends, you and me...
you brought another friend...
and then there were three...
we started our group...
our circle of friends...
and like that circle...
there is no beginning or end.

"Angel"
Heather, 7 years old.

Cold rice and cold tea are bearable, but cold looks and cold words are not.

JAPANESE PROVERB.

How beautiful what one does not understand can be!

COLETTE

We ourselves must be full of life if we are going to make life fuller for others.

DAVID SAWYER

Laughter interrupts the panic cycle of an illness.

NORMAN COUSINS

Eight Gifts of Friendship

Friends are a very rare jewel, indeed. They make you smile and encourage you to succeed. They share a word of praise.

And they always want to open their hearts to you. Show your friends how much you care. Give at least one friend one of the eight gifts of friendship today.

1. The Gift of Listening Truly listening—no interrupting, no daydreaming, no planning your response. Just listening.

2. The Gift of Affection Be generous with appropriate hugs, kisses, pats on the back, and handholds. Let these small actions demonstrate the love you have for family and friends.

3. The Gift of Laughter Clip cartoons. Share articles and funny stories. Your gift will say, "I love to laugh with you."

4. The Gift of a Note It can be a simple "Thanks for the help" note or a full sonnet. A brief, handwritten note may be remembered a lifetime, and may even change a life.

5. The Gift of a Compliment A simple and sincere, "You look great in red," "You did a super job," or "That was a wonderful meal," can make someone's day.

6. The Gift of a Favor Every day, go out of your way to do something kind.

7. The Gift of Solitude There are times when we want nothing better than to be left alone. Be sensitive to those times and give the gift of solitude to others.

8. The Gift of a Cheerful Disposition The easiest way to feel good is to extend a kind word to someone. Really, it's not that hard to say "Hello" or "Thank you."

Anonymous

The New 10 Commandments

1. Thou shall not worry, for worry is the most unproductive of all human activities.

2. Thou shall not be fearful, for most of the things we fear never come to pass.

3. Thou shall not cross bridges before you come to them, for the task is impossible.

4. Thou shall face each problem as it comes. You can only handle one at a time anyway.

5. Thou shall not take problems to bed with you, for they make very poor bedfellows.

6. Thou shall not borrow other people's problems. They can better care for them than you can.

7. Thou shall not try to relive yesterday for good or ill, it is forever gone. Concentrate on what is happening in your life and be happy now!

8. Thou shall be a good listener, for only when you listen do you hear different ideas from your own.

9. Thou shall not become bogged down by frustration, for 90 percent of it is rooted in self-pity and will only interfere with positive action.

10. Thou shall count your blessings, never overlooking the small ones, for a lot of small blessings add up to a big one.

Anonymous

Success is never a destination— it's a journey.
SATENIG ST. MARTIN

Your own stories

_____

_____

_____

_____

_____

_____

_____

_____

_____

_____

_____

_____

_____

_____

_____

_____

_____

_____

_____

_____

"Two Friends"
Jenni, 6 years old.

Afterword

Most authors don't describe the experience of writing a book as almost entirely fun. However, I can truly say that this book has been a fun-filled and enjoyable experience. I would honestly like to keep adding to the collection, but at some point I had to decide to stop.

This is the third book that I have written as a single author. I have co-authored five other publications. I believe that everyone connected with this endeavor (author, editor, layout, graphics, artwork, and readers) can say that this book is more enjoyable than stressful.

I sincerely hope that you enjoyed reading this book and that you will continue to help the publication grow by adding your own individual jokes, anecdotes, and stories.

I wish you a healthy, peaceful, and well-balanced life.

About the Author

Sue Baldwin is the owner of Insights Training & Consulting in Stillwater, Minnesota. She has owned her own company since 1994. She has been training nationally and internationally on topics related to personal and professional development since 1982. The participants in Sue's training sessions enjoy her sense of humor and informal teaching style. Her methods make it easy for participants to learn how to improve themselves and enhance their careers. Some of her topics include "What Is This Mess Called Stress," "Lighten Up and Live Longer," "Building a Better Team," "Little Spats and Huge Disputes," and "Communicating Is More Than Talking."

Sue's family consists of two adult daughters, Kris and Carrie; son-in-law Tim; grandchildren Nick and Anna; and cocker spaniel, K.C. Throughout the years she has learned to combine compassion and humor in her relationships with family, friends, colleagues, and pets.

She is avidly involved with hospice families and volunteers, and she also teaches swimming for infants and preschoolers. She has a strong grasp of the skills necessary to interact with people at all stages of living and dying. Sue's goal is to continue practicing what she preaches by lightening up and living longer.